To The
Rosen Family

"The only time
Success Comes
before Work is
in the dictionary."

"I'm blessed and honored to call Todd Durkin one of my best friends as well as a mentor and coach. He's someone who has impacted me in the greatest areas of my life, and I can promise you this: Todd Durkin and his book will get *your* mind right!"

From the foreword by **Drew Brees**, NFL quarterback
for the New Orleans Saints

"Mindset is a huge aspect of becoming a champion. Setbacks, defeats, and adversity are the things that ultimately make a champion. As someone who knows how important mental strength is in winning the game of life, I highly recommend Todd's new book *Get Your Mind Right*. I know it will help you be a champion in your life also!"

Julie Ertz, US Women's National Soccer Team;
2019 FIFA Women's World Cup champion;
2019 US Soccer Female Athlete of the Year

"I've known Todd for fourteen years, and he always brings his A game to whatever he does. His energy, passion, and positivity are contagious, and he's the kind of person who makes you better. Read this book—I know it will help you be a success in many areas of your life."

Kevin Plank, founder and former CEO of Under Armour

"Todd Durkin is one of the top performance coaches in the world. In this powerful book, he shares tips to think like a champion and habits to enhance your focus, energy, and performance. It's a must-read for anyone who wants to get their mind right and make their life great."

Jon Gordon, bestselling author of *Training Camp*
and *The Carpenter*

"Being strong means many things. You can be physically strong, mentally strong, or spiritually strong. I choose all three. I first started training with Todd Durkin five years ago to get my body stronger. What I didn't realize was that Todd trains your mind as much as he does your body. And in many ways, he touches your spirit as well. Todd's new book, *Get Your Mind Right*, is a must-read if you want to strengthen your body, mind, and soul."

Dr. David Jeremiah, senior pastor of Shadow Mountain
Community Church; founder of Turning Point Ministries

"World-class advice from a legend in the fitness industry. Now you have access to the game-changing information Todd has used to help world-class athletes and high performers get to and stay at the top of their game. It's your turn!"

JJ Virgin, nutrition and fitness expert;
New York Times bestselling author of *The Virgin Diet*

"If you've been knocked down or are struggling, or if you're simply looking to optimize your life, *Get Your Mind Right* is a must-read for you. It is rocket fuel for the soul!"

Kostas Cheliotis, cofounder, COO, and general counsel of Nassau Financial Group

"I believe that to be the best in the world at what you do requires you to have your mind right at all times. Todd Durkin and *Get Your Mind Right* will undoubtedly help you be your *best* self. I absolutely love the principles, strategies, and tactics in this book to help you win the battle between the ears."

Bo Eason, actor, playwright, and former NFL safety

"Todd's passion for life is palpable. I've known him for twenty years, and he's a man of faith, driven by purpose, and his energy is like an adrenaline injection. I love hearing and seeing how God is working through Todd in this book and know it will touch your mind and soul."

Pastor Miles McPherson, senior pastor of The Rock Church; author of *The Third Option*

"A big part of being successful in the NFL is mental strength, along with physical conditioning. For the last several years, Todd Durkin has helped me prepare physically and mentally to be my best. If you want to *Get Your Mind Right*, read this book. Just like Todd helps me prepare for life in the NFL, he can help you be your *best* also!"

Zach Ertz, NFL All-Pro tight end, Philadelphia Eagles

"Todd Durkin truly knows what it means to get your body and mind right. He's been helping the world's best athletes, executives, and high performers attain greatness for a long time. This book shares his top principles and secrets that you can now use to create maximum impact in your life also!"

Joel Marion, CEO of BioTrust Nutrition; bestselling author, speaker, and host of *Born to Impact* podcast

"I've relied on Todd Durkin for the past four years to prepare me physically and mentally for my seasons. Regardless of your age or career, there is no one better than Todd to help you take your game to the next level."

Golden Tate, NFL All-Pro wide receiver, New York Giants

"I trained with Todd Durkin for ten of my fifteen-year MLB career. One reason why I worked with him is because he always pushed me to my physical limits. But another huge reason why I worked with him is because he instilled in me a championship, winning mentality that carried over to my performance in baseball and life. I'm honored to call him a friend, and his work still greatly impacts me today. Read this book and I know it will help you whether you are an athlete, executive, parent, or someone who just wants the most out of life."

Chris Young, MLB Vice President of Baseball Operations; former MLB pitcher

"Todd Durkin has been a trainer, coach, mentor, and friend to me for over ten years. He's one of the keys that allowed me to play fifteen years in the NFL. His energy, positivity, and mindset certainly make him one of the most special coaches and people you could ever work with. Read *Get Your Mind Right* and I know Todd will help you just like he helped me."

Darren Sproles, NFL All-Pro running back, fifteen-year career

"Todd isn't just the greatest strength coach in the world, he is the most complete mind and body transformer on the planet. To be a champion, it takes much more than just the physical preparation—you must have your mind right also. Todd has a knack for helping his clients and athletes reach their personal goals through his unmatched wisdom, knowledge, energy, and mindset. Todd has impacted my life greatly, and he will impact yours too. Read this book!"

Michael Chandler, three-time MMA Lightweight Champion of the World

"I'll make this easy for you: I suffered two season-ending injuries to start my NFL career. I searched for somebody who could transform my mind and help me recover and rehab to prepare for the upcoming season. In comes Todd Durkin. He is the best in the business at 'getting your mind right.' That's why I fly out every year from Florida to California to train with him. Read this book and he will work his mental magic on you also!"

Gerald McCoy, six-time All-Pro NFL defensive tackle

"Todd Durkin epitomizes mind over matter, a true mindset warrior. I have had the pleasure of knowing Todd for more than thirty years and the honor of being his teammate in college. Todd has consistently applied the *Get Your Mind Right* approach throughout his life. This mindset resides deep in his soul. He preaches these principles to professional athletes, fitness trainers, corporate executives, and all those who look to maximize their impact in life. As a financial advisor, I see a common thread between my clients' success and the key tenets of *Get Your Mind Right*."

Tom Dexter, founder and managing partner at Commonwealth Strategic Advisory

"Few people have what it takes to not only motivate but transform lives. Todd Durkin is a force of nature. Not only will his incredible energy, spirit, and wisdom inspire you, Todd Durkin's work will help you finally make the leap from knowing what to do to embodying it. I can't recommend Todd's work enough."

Mastin Kipp, bestselling author of *Claim Your Power*; creator of Functional Life Coaching

"I've known Todd for eleven years, and I've been training with him ever since. I come out every year to San Diego not only to train my body but to get my mind right for the upcoming season. I've never met anybody like him, and he's truly the only one who knows how to get me right!"

Chase Daniel, eleven-year veteran NFL quarterback

"Todd Durkin is the king of 'get your mind right.' I've known him for ten years, I've sent numerous athletes to him, and I listen to all his content. God gave him a gift, and he's going to impact a ton of people with this book. Read this book and I know it will get your mind right . . . and then some!"

Kelli Masters, NFL agent; founder of KMM Sports

"Todd is a master teacher and motivator who not only effects positive change but also gets your mind right for the chaos of life and leadership. His teachings are truly life-changing, his words thought-provoking, and his energy infectious. No one inspires and changes lives like Todd. He will get your mind right—no matter who you are or what situation you are in."

Brad Deutser, bestselling author of *Leading Clarity*; president of Deutser management consulting firm

"I'll never forget the day that Todd sent me this crazy video of him wearing a grey hoodie and telling me to 'get my mind right' on the day of his knee surgery. I'm honored to be part of not only this book but also making his body stronger so that he can continue to do what he does so well."

Joe Jankiewicz, MD, orthopedic surgeon, Sharp Medical

"As a functional medicine MD, I value great health throughout your lifetime. One of the most important things someone can do is seek knowledge and put into practice extraordinary personal-care tools. If you are looking to improve the quality of your mind, body, and life, Todd's book is a great resource. It provides sound scientific knowledge with mindset strategies that will allow you to thrive and excel in your life."

Mona Ezzat-Velinov, ABFM, ABIHM, IFMCP, family physician in integrative and functional medicine

GET YOUR MIND RIGHT

GET YOUR MIND RIGHT

10 KEYS TO UNLOCK YOUR POTENTIAL AND IGNITE YOUR SUCCESS

TODD DURKIN

with MIKE YORKEY

BakerBooks

a division of Baker Publishing Group
Grand Rapids, Michigan

Published by Baker Books
a division of Baker Publishing Group
PO Box 6287, Grand Rapids, MI 49516-6287
www.bakerbooks.com

Printed in the United States of America

Library of Congress Cataloging-in-Publication Data
Names: Durkin, Todd, author.
Title: Get your mind right : 10 keys to unlock your potential and ignite your success / Todd Durkin.
Description: Grand Rapids, Michigan : Baker Books, a division of Baker Publishing Group, 2020. | Includes bibliographical references.
Identifiers: LCCN 2019055536 | ISBN 9780801094941 (cloth)
Subjects: LCSH: Sports—Psychological aspects. | Success. | Durkin, Todd. | Football players—United States—Biography.
Classification: LCC GV706.55 .D87 2020 | DDC 796.01/9—dc23
LC record available at https://lccn.loc.gov/2019055536

20 21 22 23 24 25 26   7 6 5 4 3 2 1

In keeping with biblical principles of creation stewardship, Baker Publishing Group advocates the responsible use of our natural resources. As a member of the Green Press Initiative, our company uses recycled paper when possible. The text paper of this book is composed in part of post-consumer waste.

green
press
INITIATIVE

To my wife, Melanie, and our children, Luke, Brady, and McKenna:

I'm sorry I wake you up screaming, shouting, and singing in the home gym before the sun comes up most mornings of the week. I just need to get my mind right!

Someday you will miss that . . . but you will always remember me.

CONTENTS

Contents

FOREWORD

by Drew Brees,
Quarterback for the New Orleans Saints

I will never forget the day I was drafted by the San Diego Chargers in the second round of the 2001 NFL draft. I recall all the preparation leading up to the draft . . . the Combine, the countless workouts and classroom interviews for multiple NFL teams, the anxiety and excitement all wrapped up into one as I anticipated where I might land to begin my NFL career.

I was projected to be a first-round pick, with six or seven teams in the mix. The Chargers were one of those teams, but unfortunately, I knew they would not be taking me with their first pick.

Here's the way the NFL draft works: the NFL takes a team's overall record from the year before and then puts all the teams in order of worst to first. And that is the order you pick. So if you had the worst record the year before, you pick first. If you were Super Bowl Champion, you pick last. There were 31 teams in 2001, so there were 31 slots in the first round. This is also the order the teams select in the second round, third round, and so on.

The Chargers had the fifth pick in the first round that year. In fact, with a record of 1–15 from the 2000 season, the Chargers actually had the first pick, but they chose to trade the pick and drop back to the fifth pick. The Chargers made a very wise move. They were able to build their roster with additional draft picks and key position players from the trade as well as draft the guy they wanted most in the first round: LaDainian Tomlinson, a heralded running back from Texas Christian University.

In the months leading up to the draft, I had many teams request individual workouts and meetings with me. This was their opportunity to dive deeper with a player they were considering drafting. Call it due diligence on their investment. The San Diego Chargers were one of those teams. I also did this for five or six other teams, all who said they would be looking to draft me in the mid to late first round. My experiences and feelings with head coach Mike Riley, offensive coordinator Norv Turner, and general manager John Butler of the San Diego Chargers were the best of all those teams.

Unfortunately, I knew they would not be taking me with the fifth pick in the draft. Their next slot was the first pick in the second round, and I would certainly be selected to another team by then. Or so I thought.

Draft Day, April 21, 2001. As I sat in my apartment with my wife-to-be, Brittany, and brother, Reid, the excitement was bubbling over. Never in my wildest dreams did I think I would be drafted to play in the NFL. It was all surreal. But which team would it be?

The Kansas City Chiefs, Jacksonville Jaguars, Miami Dolphins, Baltimore Ravens . . . these were all real contenders in the conversation to draft me. Which one would make the call? I was sure I was going to be a first-round pick. A dream come true.

Each team gets fifteen minutes to make their first-round selection, which makes for a very long process. I remember walking around the apartment, making food on the grill, playing with the dog, laughing with Brittany and Reid, just trying to get out all this nervous energy I had.

Pick after pick was made in the first round . . . and each time one of those prospective teams I mentioned was about to select, I would stand by the phone and wait for the call. But the call never came. As the first round neared an end, there was sadness and disappointment. I had been told by so many teams, scouts, coaches that if I was still available in the first round, they would be taking me!

What happened? What changed?

Then the phone rang . . . and I looked at the TV and realized which team was up next. NFL commissioner Paul Tagliabue approached the podium.

"With the first pick in the second round of the NFL Draft, the San Diego Chargers select . . . Drew Brees, quarterback, Purdue University."

My disappointment immediately turned into elation. I didn't know how this happened, but forget about the first round—this is where I really wanted to be. This is where I was meant to be. And little did I know the real *impact* this would have on my life and career.

As I write this, I am playing my nineteenth season in the NFL. Are you kidding me? What a blessing. Never in my wildest dreams could I ever imagine this reality. There have been plenty of ups and downs, ultimate achievement and bitter disappointment, adversity and sacrifice. That's why, as I look at my NFL career, there are many things I appreciate, but none more so than my relationship with Todd Durkin.

Todd has been with me every step of the way . . . from me winning back the starting QB job in 2004 after I had been benched the year before, to overcoming career-threatening injuries and disappointment, to achieving some of football's greatest accomplishments. There is no way I would have had the success, the longevity, or the joy of playing this game without Todd Durkin.

I first met Todd during the 2002 season. He was doing massage therapy and bodywork for the Chargers after our games, and I immediately took a liking to him, especially because he was a former quarterback and sensed what I needed. I could tell he really loved his craft and was passionate about the work he was doing.

In early 2004, Chargers running back LaDainian Tomlinson, who was being trained by Todd during the off-season, brought me to Fitness Quest 10 to show me Todd's functional fitness approach to training.

LT had already established himself as one of the best running backs in the league and credited his work with Todd as being a huge factor in his success. I had just finished the worst season of my career in 2003, when our team finished the year with a 4–12 record, and I had been benched three times in the process.

I was looking for every edge possible to be the best player and leader for my team. I had been told the Chargers would be bringing in another quarterback to take my job. I was not going to let that happen, but I needed help. I needed someone who could draw the best out of me, help me regain my confidence, and help take every aspect of my training and preparation to the next level. Todd would prove to be that person.

I learned very early on that training with Todd Durkin did not follow the traditional approach of lifting weights and running. Everything he had me do was fast-paced, cutting-edge, and intense. Everything we did had a purpose. Every exercise, every movement, every rep, every drill . . . from the dynamic warm-up to the multitude of high-intensity super sets to the competitions we would build into the finale of every workout.

And when I say work, I mean we WORKED! I could feel myself being sharpened and sensed my confidence growing with each session. Every day driving to his facility, I knew I had to get my mind right for what we were about to endure. But I also knew that this was the path to greatness, and there was no shortcut.

While Todd's objective was getting me into the best shape of my life from feet to fingertips, he also took a comprehensive approach to making sure he had a pulse on my mental, emotional, and spiritual well-being. He was always sharing motivational quotes, inspirational passages, and verses from the Bible to give me the right frame of mind or to put the present challenge in perspective.

I could always feel that Todd truly cared about me as a person and how I was doing in all aspects of my life. His relentless pursuit, genuine positivity, high energy, great leadership, and high character were infectious. I couldn't believe how fired up he would be every time we got together. Never had I met someone so consistent in his approach, so passionate about his calling, and so driven to make a difference, to create *impact* in people's lives.

Like I said, I've been playing in the NFL for nineteen years now. Seventeen of those years have been with Todd Durkin, and he has become one of the key fixtures in my success. It's hard to put into words what his friendship and mentorship mean to me. Undeniably he has helped me remain in the best shape of my life and continually build the mental/emotional mindset to keep me humble and hungry and playing at a high level year in and year out.

Whether it's receiving one of his crazy "Get Your Mind Right" videos from his home gym while he's working out in the early morning hours, a positive text message during a tough time, or some form of practical wisdom about how the game of life will always be bigger than the game of football, I'm blessed and honored to call Todd Durkin one of my best friends as well as a mentor and coach.

I encourage you to take heed of his advice as well as all the insights he shares. He's someone who has *impacted* me in the greatest areas of my life.

And I can promise you this . . . Todd Durkin and his book will get *your* mind right also!

FIRST QUARTER

GAME PLAN AND KICKOFF

Preparation is the key to success, and "getting your mind right" on a daily basis is imperative if you want to reach the success you desire. The principles in this book are going to help you tap into your deepest passion and your most divine purpose so that you can create the impact to make the world a better place to live.

Get fired up and get ready to play big. It's Game Time, baby!

INTRODUCTION

Get your mind right.

I've said it for more than a dozen years, and it stands for everything I do, from the time I get up until the moment I lay my head on my pillow.

Let me tell you a little bit about how I like to get up in the morning.

I don't need an alarm at 5:00 AM.

I suppose that's how I'm wired or what my body's used to, but I've always tried to beat the sun up. I've got a lot of things I want to accomplish in a day and hate losing daylight.

I spend that first half hour slowly but surely getting my mind in gear. I pray, read my Bible, and journal. Reading a portion of Scripture is my favorite way to start the day and is the best approach I know to get my mind right.

My journal is full of goals and dreams and wild ideas—just about anything that comes to mind. I also compose talks that I'm scheduled to deliver. I speak before sizable audiences forty to fifty times a year, so I'm constantly working and reworking my material. I like to be prepared when I step before a crowd. If you've ever seen me speak in public, then you know I'm always fired up to share the passions filling my heart.

I call this period of pre-dawn introspection my "quiet time." And then I'm ready for my morning workout. I own an exercise facility called Fitness Quest 10 in San Diego, California, which was named one of America's "10 Best Gyms" by *Men's Health* magazine five different times. I'm proud that the sanctuary I created twenty years ago is still thriving today.

Since I need to focus on coaching and training at Fitness Quest 10, I prefer to do many of my personal workouts in my home gym, which is actually a decked-out garage. My gym has squat racks, dumbbells, kettlebells, a bench press, an elliptical machine, and rubberized fitness flooring. I call it my "energy cave"—it's where I find the fuel for my body, mind, and spirit.

As a matter of fact, I'm so used to breaking a sweat before breakfast that I can't imagine *not* starting my day with the endorphin rush I receive from getting a good sweat. It works like magic.

But Tuesday, November 6, 2018, was a different kind of morning. Sure, I woke up at 5:00 AM on the dot, but later that morning I would be undergoing a big and scary knee surgery—a partial knee replacement.

For nine years I had a bad right knee. Bone on bone. Arthritis. Bone spurs. The last three years had been so bad that I needed to see a doctor every ninety days for cortisone shots to relieve the pain. And for the past three months, I'd been getting around on crutches because the pain and inflammation got so bad.

Life had become a living hell. I could hardly do the physical activities that most of us take for granted in life—walking across a room, standing up to shake hands, or sitting down and rising out of a chair. For a forty-seven-year-old guy who made his living in the fitness field as a trainer, traveling around the country spreading the gospel of good health and getting your mind right, not being able to walk properly was a big deal.

But all that was going to change. At 11:30 AM, I was scheduled to have a unicompartmental (or partial) knee replacement. The doctor was also going to clean up the massive arthritis in my knee and remove the bone spurs that had calcified. As scary as that was, I knew it was time to get my knee fixed.

As the procedure was explained to me, the surgeon would make a cut of three to five inches in my knee, look over the entire knee joint, and then resurface the damaged bone and tissue. When he was finished, a component made from titanium, cobalt, and high-grade plastic would be inserted into the knee and attached with bone cement. Then I'd be closed up with stitches, good to go with my new bionic knee.

One thing working in my favor was that I'd consistently trained my body during the last three years. Working around the pain, instead of doing nothing and feeling like garbage, was important. I did what I could to stay strong.

As I worked my upper body in the garage that morning, I thought about how my years of use and abuse had turned the medial part of my right knee into bone on bone, resulting in painful osteoarthritis. I'd been dealing with a compromised knee for a decade, but the last few months had been extremely difficult and painful. I couldn't go on living like this.

Believe me, I saw the irony in my need for this procedure. Besides training weekend warriors and NFL athletes, I was a motivational speaker, podcaster, author of two books, and a star in the 2016 NBC reality show called *Strong*, in which ten women from various backgrounds were paired with some of the most elite male trainers in the country. *Strong* is still airing on Netflix.

And now I had a crippling injury. I'm sure the effect was less than impressive when I worked my way to conference room podiums with a pair of crutches or wearing a brace on my knee. I hated making excuses for my weakened physical condition to an audience eager to hear my ideas about making physical and mental turnarounds.

But you know what? If I was going to come through this surgery with flying colors, I had to practice what I preached. I had to get my mind right. And that's what I did in the weeks leading up to November 6: I made a conscious decision to embrace the procedure. I was going to own it.

And there was one more thing I needed to do before my wife, Melanie, drove me to the hospital that morning. I needed to make sure that my surgeon, Dr. Joseph Jankiewicz, had his mind right too.

At the end of my early morning workout, I turned on my iPhone. Most of the time I resist the urge to turn on my smartphone—where I can get sucked into reading texts, Instagram DMs, Facebook posts, and email messages—until I've taken a shower and eaten breakfast. But that morning, a message for Dr. Jankiewicz was a priority. I wanted him to bring all his formidable skills to the operating room. I was hoping for an MVP performance.

I tapped on the camera app and thought about what I wanted to say. I was used to doing this during the NFL season when, on Game Day, I'd share an inspirational thought or two on Sunday mornings and then blast the video to a group of NFL players that I train. Today, only one person would receive my video.

I was dressed in grey sweatpants and a grey hoodie—which is my standard attire for the majority of my workouts. I held the phone in my right hand and prepped myself for a moment. Then I extended my arm, pressed the red button, and let 'er rip.

Yoo-hoo! Dr. Jankiewicz! Yeah, you know who it is! It's oh-dark thirty, baby. It's time to wake you up! IT'S GAME DAY! IT'S THE SUPER BOWL, BABY! I hope those hands are feeling like a million bucks today. I want you at your best. I'm getting my mind right, right now. I got my grey hoodie on. HEY, BROTHER, IT'S MVP DAY!

I thank you for what you do, making a difference every day, not just for me, but your entire lineup today. I pray for you, I pray for all the others, and I'M GETTING READY RIGHT NOW! I CAN'T WAIT TO SEE YOU! I'M TALKING MVP STATUS! That's what makes my soul sing.

SO GET AFTER IT, BABY! LET'S GO!

And then I ended with my signature finish—"BLAAAH!"*
Satisfied that I nailed it on one take, I attached the video and
texted this message to Dr. Jankiewicz:

> What are you doing right now? This is like the
> videos I send my NFL athletes on Game Days.
> Hope you like it!

I hit send at 6:28 AM.

Within five minutes—I kid you not—I received a reply from
Dr. Jankiewicz with a selfie of him wearing . . . a grey hoodie!
Underneath he had typed this message:

> Good to go.

I can't tell you how much the photo of him in a grey hoodie and
his three-word reply raised my spirits. I said to myself, *This guy
gets it. We see eye to eye. We have the same mindset.*

Then I remembered that I needed to do a second video, and
taping this one sobered me up like a splash of cold water. You see,
Melanie and I have three kids we adore: Luke, Brady, and McKenna.
And there was a tiny, tiny chance that I might not survive the surgery. Strange things can happen during general anesthesia, and this
crazy thing called life had taught me that nothing is guaranteed.

I learned that lesson when I suddenly lost my father to an unexpected heart attack when he was only fifty-eight. I was a tender
twenty years old at the time. While I fully expected to wake up
from my surgery, I wanted my children to have a personal message
of love and support from me—just in case things didn't work out.
You always prepare for the worst and hope for the best, right? I
told them that I loved them and tried to be the dad they always
needed and wanted.

*You can watch the video by going to YouTube and typing "Todd Durkin and
Dr. Jankiewicz" into the search bar and search for "Todd Durkin's Life Changing
Knee Surgery," MindRight Maniac Ep. 17, or go to https://www.youtube.com
/watch?v=mQkTzEkAbZE at 7:56.

After I finished recording, I heard Melanie and the kids moving about in the kitchen, grabbing breakfast before the start of the school day. I walked into the house and warmly greeted everyone, reminding myself to remember the moment.

I was physically, emotionally, and spiritually as ready as I'd ever be.

A DRIVE TO CORONADO

My surgery was scheduled at Sharp Coronado Hospital. We live in Scripps Ranch, a northern suburb of San Diego, which is about a half hour's drive from Coronado Island—technically not an island—located across San Diego Bay from downtown.

Melanie was taking the day off from Southwestern College, where she has been an exercise science professor since the late '90s. She offered to drive while I thumbed through a ton of "best wishes" and "praying for you" texts and Instagram messages sent by family members, friends, and acquaintances. In the months leading up to this day, I had been very transparent in public and on social media about my need for knee replacement surgery.

While Melanie steered us across the Coronado Bridge that spans San Diego Bay, I recalled a time in 1999 when we were crossing the same bridge.

"Melanie, I've decided to turn down the teaching position at the College of the Canyons and stay in San Diego," I had told her.

Melanie and I had met two years earlier when we were in graduate school at San Diego State. She was the attractive blonde step-aerobics instructor with great-looking legs, and I was the new weight-training and racquetball instructor graduate assistant. I always made sure that I visited her class during my breaks.

After nine months in the "friend zone," I asked her out. We had been dating for fifteen months when I received an offer from College of the Canyons, a community college in Santa Clarita just north of Los Angeles, for a full-time position as a teacher and strength and conditioning coach. Accepting would put me in a tenure track but end my budding relationship with Melanie, who'd recently accepted her own tenure-track position at Southwestern College in nearby Chula Vista.

I didn't want to lose Melanie. Before going to graduate school, I had worked for a couple years in West Los Angeles, so let's just say that I wasn't itching to return to the gridlocked freeways and the faster pace up north. At the same time, though, I recognized that I was being offered an incredible opportunity. The starting pay was significant and included full benefits with lots of room for growth.

Saying yes to College of the Canyons likely meant that I would be leaving someone very special to me—someone I could see myself marrying someday. I had a choice to make: a stable career path or a life with Melanie.

When I went to Santa Clarita and looked over the campus, it suddenly hit me what I was doing. *Oh, snap. This is serious.* I was either moving to the Los Angeles area and setting down roots or staying in San Diego to be with Melanie and seeing what job prospects developed.

I went deep in prayer, asking God which way I should go. At twenty-eight years of age, I actively sought His will in my life. After much prayer, I felt strongly that God was *not* leading me toward the comfort and security of an outstanding career opportunity in the Los Angeles area, even though I had no job and no business prospects nearby. I felt the Lord was asking me to trust Him for my future, which included Melanie.

At the highest point of Coronado Bridge on that August day in 1999, I informed Melanie that I was turning down the teaching position and staying in San Diego. "I want to take our relationship to the next level," I said. "Maybe I'll open my own fitness studio. I know I can find something to do."

Fast-forward to November 2018. As I looked down toward the deep blue bay sprinkled with a few yachts, I thought about how there had been so much, well, water under the bridge between us. I was deeply grateful to the Lord for the life He had given me. Heck, a lot had happened over the years. And I was so grateful that I had decided to turn down that job and trust my gut.

We pulled into the parking lot of Sharp Coronado Hospital, a 181-bed facility that specialized in orthopedics and joint replacement. This is where Dr. Jankiewicz performed his life-changing operations. I had done my due diligence in finding him, asking everyone I knew who was the best orthopedic doc around for knee replacements. Several sterling recommendations led me to him.

Waiting in the parking lot was a film crew hired by Sharp Hospital: two guys held video cameras, a sound guy clutched a boom, and a couple of technicians trailed the crew with clipboards. In today's connected world, the Sharp medical team and I both thought we could benefit by having a video documentation of my day of surgery. The crew filmed B-roll of me working my way on crutches from the parking lot to the hospital entrance.

Everything about Sharp Coronado was brand-spanking new and upscale. After signing my life away, I was taken to a pre-op room, film crew in tow. As the cameras whirred, two nurses attended to me: fluffing my pillow, checking my vital signs, and making sure I was comfortable in a hospital bed. We made small talk until 11:00 AM, when one of the nurses said, "I'm going to put in your IV, and it's gonna make you feel a little loopy."

So this was it. I was going under.

"Make sure you tell me when to say three, two, one," I said. I knew that anesthesia worked fast. I wanted to see if I could beat the system and make it to one before the lights went out.

I don't remember saying *three*.

INSIDE THE OPERATING ROOM

Of course, I don't recall a single thing that happened in the operating room, but I have a good idea what Dr. Jankiewicz and the

28

assisting doctors and nurses did to repair my injured knee. All I have to do is watch the forty-five-minute video.

There are shots of me lying on the operating table, tented by blue sheets, while Dr. Jankiewicz lifted my right leg and bent my knee this way and that before settling down to the business part of the operation: cutting skin and getting after my damaged knee joint.

"Can we do the center rotation of the hip and the ankle so we align the prosthesis?" Dr. Jankiewicz asked one of the nurses. He was wearing a loose gown made of a special light blue fabric, and his head was encased in a helmet and plastic visor to prevent his sweat and saliva from contaminating his incision into my knee. For all the world, it looked like he was wearing a spacesuit.

His right hand controlled a Mako robotic arm that was performing the procedure.

"This is where it's supposed to be," Dr. Jankiewicz said. The camera tightened on his face. In the background, a scratching noise that sounded like a hand grater was working on the bones inside my knee. He wasn't actually looking at my joint while he worked the robotic apparatus but had turned his attention to a monitor perched above my head.

Zzzzz . . . zzzzz . . . zzzzz.

Shades of white disappeared on the monitor screen as the Mako robotic arm shaved off the bone spurs and got after the arthritic tissue inside my medial joint.

The video cut to a shot of my head at the end of the operating table, slack-jawed and oblivious to the grinding being done in the medial compartment of my knee.

It sounded like a circular saw cutting through wood or metal, and the noise continued for half a minute—then stopped. Then there was a shot of Dr. Jankiewicz putting what looked like Elmer's glue on the back of a shiny prosthesis, followed by the sound of a hammer nailing the prosthesis into the proper place.

When he was finished, a look of satisfaction crossed Dr. Jankiewicz's face. "It's right down the pike," he said. "Looking good. It's tracking nice."

He raised my leg and bandaged knee and bent my knee back and forth again—like he was taking it for a test drive. "His knee is stable. Nice extension. Everything's spot-on."

Later, Dr. Jankiewicz told me that he'd been working with the Mako robotic arm for eight years. For the first time ever, he did not have to make one change to what the robotic arm did to me during my operation.

"You must have a guardian angel," he said. "That was the best one I'd ever seen. Normally, we have to tweak things, but the robot got it right and created the perfect knee for you."

FIRST STEPS

I'm told that I was bewildered and unsure of where I was when I came out of anesthesia. Five hours later, inside my private recovery room, one of my nurses announced that it was time to get me back on my feet. She and another nurse assistant helped me get out of bed and held my arms as I shuffled out of the room, gripping a walker with everything I had. All I had to go was ten yards down the hallway and turn around, but that distance looked as far as the horizon. I grimaced with every step, but I made it.

After a night's stay, I was released and returned home. Dr. Jankiewicz told me that I wouldn't feel like my old self for at least five weeks, but mentally I cut that time in half. That's what athletes do, right? Since I had my mind right about rehab, my recovery would be a piece of cake.

How wrong I was. Those five weeks were rough. For the first week, I stayed on the ground floor and slept in my home office on a pull-out couch. Hobbling around on a walker wasn't a picnic. And I could forget about driving: I wouldn't be allowed to get behind the wheel for at least five weeks because my knee that went under the knife was the one that operated the gas pedal and brake. We wouldn't take that chance.

Housebound, I decided to make the most of this "time out" from life. At the start of 2018, I had written in my journal about taking a sabbatical to refresh and recharge. Perhaps I, along with the family, could rent a home in the Rocky Mountains. That never happened, but it slowly dawned on me that I had been handed a unique opportunity: five weeks with not a whole lot to do but rehab my knee.

This was the start of five weeks of intense physical rehabilitation exercises and personal introspection. I used my time to journal, pray, and think about how God could use these weeks to change me and bring me closer to His will.

You choose change or change chooses you.

Those five weeks were powerful. I was mentally all-in on the healing process. I was all-in listening to the whispers of what God was telling me during that time. I recognized that this "alone time" might not ever happen to me again.

In my journal, I tackled questions like these:

- What am I supposed to do with this partial knee replacement surgery?
- Will I regain my strength and walk normally again?
- How can I use this experience to impact more people?

Journaling played a huge part in my healing and getting my mind right for the next stage in my life.

These days, I can't tell you how great I feel. Submitting to a partial knee replacement procedure was one of the smartest decisions I ever made. Before I went under the knife, I was massively bowlegged and walked around like a cowboy who just got off a horse, but the partial knee replacement procedure took out seven degrees of my bowleggedness. I can walk without pain and even jog, but I'm leaving the distance running to others. There are a thousand ways to stay in great shape without pounding the pavement.

I'll be the first to admit that getting my mind right was a process, but now that I'm on the other side, I'm jacked up about helping others make the physical, mental, emotional, and spiritual changes they need to lead better lives.

So many people don't have their mind right today. I see it in the young people who are defeated when they don't get hundreds of likes on their latest Instagram post. I see it in young parents struggling to keep all the balls in the air. I see it in older folks shuffling toward the great unknown of retirement. Their bodies are breaking down, and their bank accounts are evaporating.

On top of that, there's the stress on our souls during these turbulent times. All you have to do is look at the school and workplace shootings, the natural disasters, the latest political scandals, and unrest around the world to see how screwed up things are.

So how can you get your mind right in the midst of all these challenges?

In the following pages, I'll be sharing ten keys to smack fear in the face, ignite your energy, and dominate your life. I'm going to personally coach you and give you the tools necessary to catapult your body, mind, and spirit into a different stratosphere.

Are you with me? Will you commit to making a change? I'm ready to go if you are because I want to fix the world.

Don't laugh. I believe that if I can inspire people to take steps to make their minds right, then we're all going to be better off.

But Todd, you might say, *I'm not in a good place. I'm still figuring things out.*

That's okay. Getting your mind right doesn't happen as easily as flipping a light switch. A good place to start is repeating a mantra that I often share with the professional athletes I work with: *Control the controllables and stop worrying about things you can't change.* I'm surprised by how many times I have to remind others—and myself—that we're better off when we put our time and energy into the things that we can control.

So what can you control?

The hours that you're awake and going through life. How you interact with others. Where you focus your time. Who you choose to spend your time with. What you listen to. What you watch. What you eat. How much you exercise. And a zillion other things. I want to inspire you to have a new mindset regarding everything you do during the precious hours from when you wake until the moment you lay your head on your pillow at night.

Perhaps your mind is not where it should be right now. Hey, we're all on a journey, but are you noticing what's happening around you as you go through life? Or are you going to let two, three, five, or ten years pass without doing anything, without coming up with a plan, without taking control of your life?

There's a little saying that's inspired me over the years, and it's this:

If it's going to be, it's up to me.

If it's going to be, then it's up to you. There's nothing like choosing the present to change your mindset.

It's time to get your mind right.

KEY #1

Dream Big—
and Attack Your Fears!

Life ain't about how hard ya hit. It's about how hard
you can get hit and keep moving forward. How much
you can take and keep moving forward. That's how
winning is done.

—Rocky Balboa, legendary character
of the *Rocky* films

In the mid-2000s, a new TV show caught fire: *The Biggest Loser*.

The reality program featured morbidly obese and seriously over-weight individuals competing against each other to lose the highest percentage of weight relative to their initial weigh-in. The "con-testants" were divided up into teams that worked with personal trainers who dished out sadistic workouts with the empathy of a drill sergeant. Each episode produced plenty of cringe-worthy moments, like when the corpulent contestants walked past glass-fronted "temptation refrigerators" brimming with donuts, cakes, pies, pizza, and beer.

Season after season, *The Biggest Loser* was ratings gold for NBC, drawing around 10 million viewers a week and spawning spin-offs like *Extreme Weight Loss, My Diet Is Better Than Yours, I Used to Be Fat,* and *Shedding for the Wedding.* As I watched these shows parade by, I wondered if I would ever get a shot at being a trainer on one of these weight-loss TV programs.

I knew I could do a great job inspiring those seeking to shed pounds. I've always said that a weight-loss regimen is much more than consuming fewer calories and exercising more. There's a mental and spiritual side that must be addressed as well. But I rarely saw that aspect on TV!

For years, I made participating in a health-related reality show one of my big, hairy, audacious goals, or what I call a BHAG. If the stars aligned one time and the opportunity came my way, I would go for it. Every January, when I finished my Annual Roadmap & Strategic Plan for the coming year, I included this presumptuous goal on my list.

I had no idea how to make this happen. Except for Michael King, I didn't know anyone in Hollywood. I didn't train actors or producers. I trained pro athletes and everyday weekend warriors and fitness enthusiasts. So after nine years of including "Be on a TV show and have a global impact" on my list, I didn't write it down shortly after New Year's Day in 2015. It wasn't happening.

A month later, though, what do you think happened? I received a phone call out of the blue from a production company in Hollywood. An assistant introduced herself and said she was working on a new show that would pair ten of the top trainers in America with ten female contestants who wanted to change their lives. These women would be interested in losing more than a few inches off their waistlines; they also wanted to change their mental outlook and become better people.

That sounded like something in my wheelhouse.

"You've been identified as someone that we would potentially like to have on our show," the production person said. "We'd like to come down to San Diego, meet you, see you in action."

"This is fantastic. So how did you hear about me?"

"We talked to a few people, and your name consistently came up in coaching circles as someone who has high energy and would be great on TV. We checked you out on YouTube, and you're definitely a guy we want to talk to."

The following week, she and another production assistant arrived at my gym to watch me put clients through the paces. They liked what they saw.

A couple of months passed with intermittent contact with this production assistant. Each time I heard from her, though, she was optimistic. "If the show's going to happen, we want you to come up to LA for an audition," she said.

Audition? What was there to audition about?

"I don't know why you guys need me to audition, but I'll be more than happy to. But what you saw is who I am," I said.

The next thing I knew, I found myself in a hotel ballroom near downtown LA, positioned before a dozen or so executive producers, "auditioning" for the role. I looked out into darkness while several bright lights shone on me. The producers were creating a stagelike atmosphere. Would I crumble under the lights, or would I light up? Would I get flustered and flounder, or would I be dialed in?

I wasn't going to let the situation get too big for me. When a voice in the darkness asked me why I wanted to be on the show, I was ready.

"Not only will you not find a trainer more dedicated than me, but I believe my purpose on this earth is to change people's lives. When it comes to mindset, I don't believe there are any other coaches on the planet who are more passionate, more positive, or more energetic in a genuine and authentic way. I want to be part of something that will not only change one person's life but millions of lives as well."

I spoke confidently, not in a boastful manner or in a way that could be construed as putting down other candidates. That said,

37

I'd been in the fitness space for twenty years and knew that changing people's lives involved a lot more than working them out with kettlebells, free weights, and TRX suspension trainers; I knew that people change from the inside out. I had to get their minds right.

I never saw the value in just pounding people and pulverizing them, like those trainers on *The Biggest Loser*. I said to the producers, "My mission is to change the body, mind, and soul of whoever I come in contact with. I don't care if she is twenty years old or a fifty-five-year-old grandmother. I will do everything in my power to transform the way she thinks, acts, lives, and believes. And I guarantee it!"

ON THE SHORT LIST

When my audition was over, one of the producers called and told me that they had brought in dozens of trainers for the audition, and I was on their short list. It felt like I was part of an *American Idol* competition where a panel of judges held my fate in their hands.

I did gain some important intel during the audition. The production company behind the new reality show was 25/7 Productions, headed by David Broome, the producer of *The Biggest Loser*. When Broome introduced himself to me in Los Angeles, I knew all the talk was legit. Then he mentioned that Sylvester Stallone— yup, my hero, Rocky—was an executive producer. This show was destined for network TV. Stallone, the father of three young adult daughters—Sophia, Sistine, and Scarlet—said he wanted to be part of a reality show that helped female competitors reach their full potential.

A week later, Broome's assistant called me again. "Listen, you crushed it in the audition," she said. "If this show goes and gets picked up by a network, there's a 99 percent chance you'll be on."

That was great news. But I was thinking, *What's the other 1 percent?*

I heard the same message from 25/7 Productions throughout the summer of 2015: *Things look great. You're 99 percent there.*

After the third or fourth time I heard I was 99 percent there, I flat-out asked the production assistant what the 1 percent chance was all about.

"I'm glad you brought that up," she said. "We've been looking at your health history, and we've noticed that your dad passed away at the age of fifty-eight from a heart attack. Since you have a history of heart disease in the family, you'll have to pass our physical. That's the 1 percent we're talking about."

I've been through several physical examinations by medical personnel in the past, but the one Broome's team put me through was extreme—something a high-level executive or Navy SEAL would have to endure. As part of my physical, I had to drive to Cedars-Sinai Medical Center in Los Angeles to undergo a stress test on a treadmill that would get progressively more difficult and then submit to a nuclear heart scan in which I swallowed a radioactive dye and then lay in an imaging machine that took pictures of my cardiovascular system, looking for areas of poor blood flow or damage to the heart vessel.

Apparently, I checked out just fine. In fact, I had a beautiful heart with no plaque buildup or blockages in my heart valves.

On an August afternoon, Broome's assistant called again. "Congratulations. We'd like you to be one of the trainers on the show."

"Sweet," I said. It looked like my BHAG was happening. "What exactly will I be doing?"

"You'll be training and coaching your gal, and together you'll be competing to win $500,000. There will be ten trainers and ten women."

"How long will I be training her?" I was figuring a month or so to tape the shows.

"Upward of three months, if you keep winning. And you'll be sequestered the entire time when you're not on set. You will have little contact with the outside world."

What? It slowly dawned on me that network reality shows involved much more time and sacrifice than I could have imagined. Was I doing the right thing? Several questions weighed heavily on my heart:

Am I truly counting the cost?

Do I really need to do this show?

Am I doing this purely for ego?

I had good reason to be concerned. I might have to leave Fitness Quest 10 for up to three months. Not only that, I wouldn't be allowed to have any communication with my trainers and team at the gym.

Wow—was this something I really should do?

I had forty-two employees in my business. I had a book of clients. I coached a Mastermind group of trainers—around 200— once a month via video conferencing. None of that could happen while I was competing.

And what would be the financial hit I'd take? Sure, the producers would be giving me a per diem, but that nominal sum wasn't even close to what I usually took in each week. I worried that the financial risk was too big.

The biggest fear, though, was this: What would happen to my family while I was gone for up to three months? Contact between us would be extremely limited. I couldn't speak to Melanie or the kids except for a one-hour "phone visit" on Sunday afternoons. Prison inmates had better visiting hours.

A third major issue was my contract with Under Armour. In 2006, I signed a sponsorship agreement with the sports apparel company to exclusively wear Under Armour. Fitness Quest 10 was the first Under Armour–sponsored training facility in the world.

Under Armour's founder, Kevin Plank, had become a good friend. Over the years, he asked me to speak at Under Armour events held at the Super Bowl, Pro Bowl, and other major sporting venues around the world. My contract specified that when I was in a fitness setting, I had to be decked out in Under Armour from head to toe. The trouble was that I had no idea what sports apparel we would be wearing on the show.

When I called Kevin to explain my dilemma, he couldn't have been more gracious. "If this show is going to help your career, then go for it. Make it your time to shine and make us proud," he said.

Being out of pocket for up to three months also meant that I would have to cancel a three-and-a-half-day mentorship event that I host annually for fitness pros and entrepreneurs looking to build their business, improve their leadership skills, and attain personal growth. My mentorship event is my deepest and most intense live gathering of the year, and I only do one every fall. Around one hundred people would be paying $2,000 each, so we had a six-figure budget.

When the show's assistant producer said they wanted me, though, I already had a nonrefundable hotel contract in place. I'd have to forfeit a down payment of $32,000. On top of that, thirty-two people had signed up early and booked flights to San Diego. If I moved back the mentorship conference by five or six months, the honorable thing to do would be to pay the change fees for their flights.

I approached the producers of the show about having to swallow a $32,000 deposit for hotel lodging. Was there anything they could do?

They told me I was out of luck.

"Take it or leave it," I was told.

I lost the deposit.

NO GUARANTEES

I learned that the name of the show was *Strong*, and it would be part of the NBC lineup, the same network that televised *The Biggest Loser*.

But there was no guarantee that *Strong* would ever air! We could be doing weeks of filming for nothing if NBC decided they didn't like the way the show turned out. That raised more fear in my heart.

How would I perform with that prize of up to $500,000 in sight? I was forty-four years old with heavy-duty mileage on the odometer. My right knee was bothering me; ditto for my right shoulder. Although I didn't know this for sure, I suspected that I would be competing against jacked trainers a decade or two younger than me. I could get smoked the first week and be sent home.

The other issue was how I would come across on flat-screen TVs across America. I'd heard horror stories about reality shows—how the show's producers could make you look like a fool in an instant, depending on how they "edited" the episodes, and there would be nothing I could do about it. This was spelled out in the contract I signed.

When I lumped together my fears, the scales tipped toward playing it safe and saying "thanks, but no thanks" to the *Strong* producers at the last minute. But then another thought crept into my mind—another saying I had repeated to my students and clients over the years: *Sometimes you have to give up the good to get to the great.*

If that was the case, then I'd have to attack my fears like I did in everyday life. Sure, I had a comfortable existence, a great family, a thriving business, and the respect of my peers. But now something inside of me was saying, *Hey, if you want to go to a deeper level, if you want to challenge yourself, you're going to have to do this. It's going to involve running at your fears. You're going to have to give up a lot.*

I had to get comfortable with the idea of being uncomfortable for the first time in years, dating back to the time when I said no to taking that professorship at College of the Canyons. I ran through a wall of fears to open Fitness Quest 10 with no clients, no business plan, and very little money, but I was sure glad I did.

Since I always wanted to be a trainer on a reality TV show—and now the opportunity was staring at me smack in the face—why was I entertaining doubt? Why did I have fears about looking bad in front of others? Why couldn't I get my mind right on this? The fear of failure has a scientific name: *atychiphobia*. We are under its power whenever fear stops us from taking on challenges that can move us forward to achieve our goals and objectives. I see fears of all kinds every day:

- Professional athletes who fear getting cut in training camp.
- Moms who fear they'll never lose the weight they gained during pregnancy.
- Golf nuts who suffered their first major injury and wonder if they'll ever swing a club again.
- Teens with low self-esteem who hate suiting up for gym class.
- Millennials who are afraid of how other people are judging them on social media.

I see fear and defeat on the faces of new clients when they come into my gym for the first time. Here's a typical interchange that I've had hundreds of times over the years at Fitness Quest 10:

Me: Hi, Bill. Welcome! I'm glad you're here for our first appointment. Why are you here today?

Bill: Todd, I know I need to do something about my weight. My dad died from type 2 diabetes right after he turned sixty. I'm in my thirties, and I've got a couple of young kids. I'm worried that I'm on the same route as him. This is hard for me to admit, but I think I need to lose some weight.

Me: Why do you need me to be your trainer?

Bill: Because what I'm doing is not working.

Me: Why isn't it working?

Bill: Well, all you have to do is take one look at me.

Me: When I look at you, I'm looking at your outside, but I don't see your inside. What do you see when you look at yourself?

Bill: Well, I see someone who weighs way too much. It bothers me.

Me: Why does it bother you?

Bill: Because I know I'm not healthy. I can't be living healthy, not at this weight.

Me: So ultimately you're searching for your best health?

Bill: Yeah, I am. That's why I'm here today. I hope you can help me.

Look closer at this interchange between Bill and me. I asked him "why" questions five times until I got to the core and essence of why Bill made an appointment with me: He wants to feel better. He wants to be healthier so he can have a stronger relationship with his wife and be a better dad to his kids. He didn't come to my gym just because of the extra hundred pounds on his frame. He came to recapture his health, his vitality, and his energy. Now I knew what buttons I could push to help him get there.

I started coaching him right then:

Me: Let me tell you, it's not going to be easy. Getting healthy involves change and changing habits. But I'm going to be there for you, asking questions that will hold you accountable. Sure, we're going to train together three days a week, but there are another twenty-three hours in each day that you can use to your benefit. You'll not only be choosing what you eat, but you'll also be choosing what you read. I'm going to text you some inspirational quotes to help you get your mind right. Because it sounds like you've fallen out of love with yourself.

How are you going to love your wife and kids when you can't love yourself? That's what I want to help you with. Are you ready to get started today?

Bill: I'm ready, Todd. It was scary for me to come here today. I didn't think I'd ever do this, but I'm here.

Me: It is scary, so I applaud you. You actually made the hardest step, which is the first step, and that was admitting to yourself that you want to get better, that you have a problem, and that you can't do it alone. You're just like the pro athletes who come to me. They want motivation, accountability, and my know-how of what it takes to get to the next level.

You're of the same mindset. I can tell that you're looking to become the best version of yourself, period. You called me and then walked into something I call my sanctuary. For you, it'll probably be a torture chamber, but you're going to learn to love it and you're gonna learn that at any time, whenever you're facing tough times in your life, in your business, in your career, you could always turn and realize that you got your physical health.

Sure, you may have had great success in other areas of life, but there's always another level. Today, you made the most difficult step. We're about to go out there and start training, so keep this thought in your mind: those who have their health have a thousand dreams. Those who don't have nothing.

For the next hour, we're going to train and we're going to sweat. We're going to get your heart rate up, and we're going to build muscle. We're going to build more than physical muscle—we're going to build mental muscle and spiritual muscle. I want to build up every aspect of you so that you can physically, mentally, and spiritually go out there and be the best person you can possibly be. When that happens, then you're living your divine purpose as well. Let's get out there and get after it.

Did you need to hear that pep talk?

I needed to hear a different kind of pep talk regarding *Strong*. My fears centered on whether I was doing the right thing being gone so long from my family; how I'd fare against younger, stronger PTs; and if I'd make a fool of myself on national TV. So I did what I do with all my clients. I gave myself some coaching.

Sure, there are risks going on Strong, *but walking away from the challenge will set you up for a lifetime of regret. If you don't try, you will never know. If you never know, it's because you didn't try.*

What about you? Do you want to be the person who said to himself or herself, *I wish I would have tried. I wish I could have trusted myself to take that risk.*

Listen, we've all been there, but the answer is clear. You don't want to live a life of regrets, even if the risk of failure is there. You want to get your mind right, jump headfirst into the unknown, and win the day.

GETTING STRONGER

On the drive to Los Angeles, I was filled with two emotions: excitement and fear. I didn't really know what I was getting into. I checked into a hotel in Woodland Hills—part of San Fernando Valley—where I saw the other trainers, but we weren't allowed to speak to each other. I was given a room key—and told I would be allowed out of my room for one hour a day to work out.

This went on for ten days! The experience started feeling like a jail sentence very quickly to me, complete with meals delivered to my "cell." The only difference was that the food was excellent; the show producers had chosen their caterer well. But even eating nutritious meals by myself in a hotel room got monotonous quickly. I was lonely and missed my family. I would later learn that we were being sequestered for so long because the set wasn't ready yet.

Instead of watching movies or catching up on my reading all day, I decided to start writing my second book, which I would call *The WOW Book: 52 Ways to Motivate Your Mind, Inspire Your Soul & Create WOW in Your Life.* I didn't finish the book in ten distraction-free days, but I made a solid start.

And then one evening, I was told to pack my bags and meet in the lobby. When I stepped out of the elevator that evening, I saw the other trainers gathering around a *Strong* assistant. None of the women competing on *Strong* were there, however.

"Listen up, everybody," announced a production assistant. "We're on 'hard ice,' and that means you're not allowed to talk to each other. Thank you for your cooperation."

Hard ice? What's going on here? I was eager to chat up the guys rocking back and forth on their heels, who were cut from the same personal trainer cloth as me. After all, we were thrown into the same pond of reality TV, right? Why couldn't we speak to each other?

We stepped into a fifteen-passenger van and rode in silence into the coastal foothills between the San Fernando Valley and Malibu. I knew the area well: before I met Melanie, I was a personal trainer to the stars there when I was in my midtwenties. A Hollywood kingpin named Michael King hired me as his personal trainer and massage therapist. You've probably never heard of Michael, who was the CEO of King World Productions, but you've heard of the shows his company produced: *Oprah, Wheel of Fortune,* and *Jeopardy!*

Michael had taken me under his wing when I was a broken-down quarterback, severely injured while playing in the European Football League. I was wondering what I was going to do next in life when Michael asked me to do massage and bodywork therapy for his back, along with some personal training. He immediately liked me and my work.

The next thing I knew, I was moving to Los Angeles and living in Michael's guest house in Malibu. I'm talking about a guest house on a beautiful beachfront property owned by the pop singer Sting. Those memories came flooding back to me as I sat in the *Strong* van. Even though it was dark outside, I immediately recognized the hilly terrain of Topanga Canyon Boulevard, the main link between Woodland Hills and Malibu.

We arrived at a woodsy resort that looked like a "fat farm," one of those rustic yet luxurious places where rich people eat healthy, lose weight, and traipse from one spa experience to another. I noticed several low-slung wooden buildings around a nice pool with a common-area meeting place. Everything was decorated quite tastefully.

Upon arrival, the other trainers and I gathered in the meeting room for a briefing.

"Tonight, you'll meet your future partner as well as the host of the show, who will explain what's going on," the production assistant said. "Remember, everything will be filmed, so act like you don't know the cameras are there."

When she said "tonight," she wasn't kidding. The other trainers and I went to our rooms and were sequestered there until 11:00 PM, when we boarded a van—still under "hard ice" conditions—for a ten-minute drive to the "arena."

I'm not saying that it was past my bedtime, but eleven o'clock was rather late for a grueling workout. No matter. I was psyched and ready as the van traveled along a windy two-lane road deep into the foothills of Malibu.

Out of the pitch darkness, I saw a ring of bright lights illuminating the black sky—kind of like when the spaceship lands in the Spielberg flick *Close Encounters of the Third Kind*. Now this was getting interesting.

The nighttime air of late September was chilly. Underneath our parkas, we were dressed in black training apparel with a *Strong* logo and our first names printed above the heart. We were taken behind a stage, where we were told to run out when we heard our name called.

So that's what I did. When I hit the brightly lit stage, I saw three hundred cameras aimed at me from the corner of my eye. Maybe I exaggerate, but not by much.

Wow. This is real.

On one side of the stage stood ten trainers, all male. On the other side, lined up shoulder to shoulder, were ten women who looked to be in their late twenties and thirties. They were dressed in black workout tights and different-colored tops—white, blue, orange, purple, grey, yellow, olive, red, aqua, and lime. I heard a voice over a loudspeaker announce: "We now welcome your host, professional volleyball player and fitness expert Gabrielle Reece!"

I knew exactly who she was from her volleyball days. She'd hosted *Insider Training* on the Discovery Channel, been part of ESPN's *Gravity Games*, and written a *New York Times* bestseller: *My Foot Is Too Big for the Glass Slipper*. And Gabby was married to pro surfer Laird Hamilton, the big-wave rider whose American Express commercials showing him being towed into massive swells made him an international celebrity.

"Welcome, everyone, to *Strong*, where ten of America's top trainers are paired with ten trainees, and together they will compete for up to $500,000," Gabby said.

Yikes. I've got my hands full, and we haven't even started. Glancing to my right and left, I spotted several young, chiseled guys with ripped muscles busting out of their *Strong* shirts. Most of them appeared to be ten to twenty years my junior. I looked like a healthy, average dad competing against a bunch of built guys who stepped off an NFL training field.

They put the trainers to the test immediately. We would take a sledgehammer to a short stack of cinder blocks. Break that, and there was a rope for the next task, which would be used to pull a heavy weight up a tower . . . you get the idea.

What the producers didn't know was that I had a lion inside my heart. I started swinging that heavy sledgehammer like a banshee and finished fifth—the middle of the pack.

The women were then told to pick the trainer they wanted to work with. They were randomly selected to see who would pick first.

Jill May, a mom of four and a pastor's wife in her midthirties, picked the first-place finisher from our group: Bennie Wylie, a former strength and conditioning coach for the Dallas Cowboys. He had the entire package: an intimidating physique, a thunderous voice, a cool-looking goatee, and a bald head. He looked to be in his late thirties. I liked Bennie and what he stood for, but man, was he a beast.

Victoria Castillo, a wedding photographer, chose Leyon Azubuike, who appeared to be every inch the heavyweight boxer that he said he was. Sarah Miller, a Chicago writer, tabbed Drew Logan, a celebrity trainer from Manhattan Beach, California. Devon Cassidy, a twenty-four-year-old professional from the Boston area, chose next and picked me, probably because I finished fifth. It certainly wasn't because I was some jacked-up, chiseled young dude.

But the trainers weren't allowed to talk to our trainees. "We're still on hard ice, everybody," said a voice in the shadows. When we stopped filming, it was 2:00 AM. We were driven back to our living quarters. And so it began.

During my stint on *Strong*, I learned a few things about reality TV. The reason why the producers want "hard ice" conditions is because they want to capture every conversation between the trainers and the trainees. The next morning, with the cameras rolling, we met at an outdoor/indoor fitness area that was called the Strong Yard. This is where we would do our training during the entire show.

I watched Devon, a tallish blonde, tell the camera, "I'm Devon, and I'm from Boston, Massachusetts. I'm a young professional with a lot going on in my life. But I'm not really happy with a lot of the areas because my mom and dad are in the midst of a divorce. I'm searching for my deeper purpose in life, and I don't like to compete."

Wait, did she just say she doesn't like to compete? Whoa—this is going to be a problem!

THE ELIMINATION TOWER

The producers came up with a series of physical challenges each week. The winner could choose a team to go to the Elimination Tower, a neon-lit four-story edifice containing eight nasty tests of brute strength, power, endurance, and agility. They would compete against the team that finished last in a previous challenge. The losing team from the Elimination Tower went home.

The first time we saw the Elimination Tower—in the middle of the night—jaws dropped. I just smirked. I looked at everyone and said, "This ain't no Elimination Tower. This is the Opportunity Tower."

"That's an interesting perspective," one of the trainers said.

I was trying to get my mind right. I knew that sooner or later our team was going to the Elimination Tower. I wanted to look at that monster as an opportunity to stay in the game—not to go home.

Devon and I found ourselves at the "Opportunity Tower" sooner than expected. In Week 3, we lost a dual bench press challenge that involved lifting a log filled with water, which sent us to the Elimination Tower against another team.

Two hours before the Elimination Tower, Devon suffered a major panic attack. "There's no way I'm doing the Elimination Tower," she cried out.

I did my best to settle her and get her mind right.

"I don't care if we lose this competition, but we're going in and we're going to compete," I said. "What are you going to look like to your friends back in Boston when this show airs and they announce that you quit? There's absolutely a zero chance that you're quitting."

My words didn't help. Her panic attack continued to the point where the medical team was called in. A doctor checked her out and was able to calm her down with breathing exercises. Thank God she rallied and was able to go.

In this case, GO time was midnight. The first obstacle involved making a running start and jumping onto a wishbone-shaped, tackling-dummy-like bag. We had to hang on for dear life and safely slide ten yards to the other side. In the two previous Elimination Tower competitions, I saw how the women had trouble hanging on to the bag long enough to cross a ten-yard moat because of their lack of upper-body strength.

Sure enough, Devon kept sliding off the bag. After a dozen attempts, I said to myself, *Screw it. The next time we jump on the bag, I'm going to pin her to the bag with my right arm.* My strategy worked and we got to the other side, but I felt something pop in my right shoulder when I pinned her to the bag. With adrenaline running high, though, I kept going.

Meanwhile, the other team made steady progress up the tower and beat us handily. We lost and were eliminated, but I was proud of my effort as well as Devon's. Lord knows, she tried, and that's all I wanted her to do—compete.

Even though I would no longer be on the show, I thought I had to stick around, much like how *Survivor* contestants who've been eliminated kick back on the "Ponderosa" until filming is completed. Instead, one of the producers pulled me aside.

"Hey, Todd, we understand that you've got a family. You've got a business to run. We're going to keep the losing women here, but you have the option to go home."

Based on my desire to see my family and my responsibilities at Fitness Quest 10, I decided that it was time to go home after being on the set for five weeks. During the two-and-a-half-hour drive back to San Diego the next morning, I thought about how I had dreamed big and realized a big, hairy, audacious goal. I had been part of a national TV show that showcased physical trainers helping others turn their lives around through tough physical work, eliminating mindless carbs, and getting your focus right. I had successfully run at my fears. Frankly, I felt like I had conquered them.

But all that was in my rearview mirror. On the car ride home, I realized what was more important than successfully running at my fears, and that was my family.

They would make my mind right after my early elimination from *Strong*.

After all, family is where I had been finding my strength for my entire life.

KEY #2

Your Thoughts Ultimately Determine Your Legacy

Make sure your worst enemy doesn't live between your own two ears.

—Laird Hamilton, big wave surfer

I grew up the youngest of eight in an Irish-Catholic family in a small New Jersey coastal town known as Brick Township. We lived in a suburban ranch house on Edgewood Drive. With so many kids running in and out of our front door, our home became the neighborhood's gathering place.

My sister Karen was just a year older than me. Her best friend was Susan Schnabel, who lived just two blocks away. They would let me play kickball with them when I was in kindergarten and first grade, which made me feel grown up. I never could have imagined then, as a kid trying to keep up, that I'd one day inspire Susan during one of the most difficult times of her life.

Susan was in her early thirties when she fell in love with Scott Fairgrieve, who had a son from a previous marriage. After they married, Susan embraced her new role as a stepmom.

In 2011, after six years of marriage, Scott turned forty-one and was putting on weight too easily. He decided to take action and hire a personal trainer to help him get in shape. I would have loved to work with him, but that wasn't going to happen since I was living in San Diego.

At the same time, Susan decided to do something totally different and start a small business she called the Coastal Collection. Featuring her photography of coastal elements—starfish, seashells, ropes, beachscapes, lighthouses, and nautical components—she developed a product line that she showed at local art galleries.

Then, out of nowhere, Scott suffered a major heart attack on October 12, 2012. Doctors performed an angioplasty to open the blocked vessels that supplied blood to his heart to save his life. After this major surgery, Scott started rehab.

Scott kept up his rehab program, taking the right medications and continuing a new exercise program—all the things that a heart attack victim is supposed to do. He made steady progress, and then on his forty-second birthday, December 28, he and Susan visited friends in Cape May and got home late that night.

Early the next morning, he woke Susan out of a deep sleep. He had a backpack over his shoulder, which struck her as strange.

"I need you to take me to the hospital," he said.

Now Susan was wide awake. She rushed him to the local emergency room, where doctors checked him out and ran all sorts of tests. Throughout the day, Scott was closely monitored.

That night, at 8:30, the nursing staff informed Susan that she should go home and get some rest. Shortly after she departed, Scott suffered another heart attack. This time he didn't pull through. Scott Fairgrieve died on December 29, 2012, just one day after his forty-second birthday.

Susan was absolutely devastated. Some days, she couldn't force herself to get out of bed or shower. She kept the blinds closed and refused to leave the house on occasion. Since her stepson, Scott Jr., was with his mom, she was in a really dark and lonely place.

Months and months passed, and Susan was still in the grip of the depression.

During those dark days, she thought about me. She found my YouTube channel and watched videos of me speaking before various audiences. She was particularly drawn to my message of having the right mindset in life—that everything we do and everything we are stems from the way we think about ourselves and the world around us. Even amidst all the darkness, if she could get her mind right, Susan could focus more clearly on her purpose. She could reclaim her dreams for the future and cherish her relationships with family and friends.

What really caught her attention was when I spoke about "getting 1 percent better each day"—chipping away and scoring small victories until she experienced the breakthrough. My positivity was what she needed to move forward during a very difficult time.

Susan was inspired to eventually join a gym, where she started working with a personal trainer. Each time she threw a ten-pound medicine ball to the ground with as much energy as she could muster, she believed she was getting 1 percent better that day. She told friends, "When you think you cannot do one more, you can do three!"

On July 16, 2016, three and a half years after Scott's death, Susan was working in her garage on her Coastal Collection business on an extremely hot day. She recalled the happy times when she and Scott vacationed on the tiny, isolated island of Nantucket, Rhode Island, thirty miles off the coast of Cape Cod, Massachusetts.

Suddenly, the perfect logo occurred to her, out of the blue, like a gift from above: ACK 4170—ACK was the airport code for Nantucket Memorial Airport, and 4170 represented the geographical coordinates: 41 longitude and 70 latitude. From that day forward, her new venture was called ACK 4170. After launching a website in the spring of 2017, the response was so great that Susan felt confident to take the huge step to move to Nantucket and open a retail store in the historic downtown district. ACK 4170 has since won numerous storefront contests and was voted "Best Nantucket Gift Shop."

"I'm glad I have my mind right about the challenges of owning a brick-and-mortar business in a vacation area because running ACK 4170 has been a tougher journey than I ever anticipated," Susan said. "I thank Todd for being a constant positive role model and mentor during my darkest days. He's also been a great help to my widows' support group in New Jersey. They continue to use his positive messages and make out their annual roadmaps in their January meeting. Needless to say, Todd has made a huge impact on us all."

Susan Schnabel Fairgrieve is an example of someone who had to get her mind right under the toughest of experiences—losing a spouse at a young age. There are many challenges in life where having the right mental outlook is paramount, such as times of financial distress, a life-changing injury, or the loss of a dream. Perhaps you've dealt with one or all of these things. I know I have, and I can easily think of more examples from clients and friends.

There was the client at Fitness Quest 10 who told me that he and his family were $10,000 behind in their mortgage payments and would surely lose their home. There was a leader on my management team, Julie Wilcox, whose life changed the moment her husband, Gary, suffered a serious stroke. And there was my close friend Trina Gray, who called me just hours after her daughter Jade blew out her ACL playing high school volleyball in Michigan, potentially dashing her dreams of playing Division 1 volleyball.

The common denominator for each of them was the desire to have the right mindset moving forward. So much happens between the ears, as I often heard my football coaches say through the years, which is why the first thing I want you to tackle is your thought life.

THOUGHTS BOUNCING AROUND OUR HEADS

"For as he thinks in his heart, so is he," wrote King Solomon, the wisest man who ever lived, in Proverbs 23:7 (NKJV). This leads right into my first key for keeping your mind right:
Your thoughts determine your life and your legacy.
Have you ever thought about what you're thinking? You should, you know. Some researchers claim that the average person has around 70,000 thoughts a day, which may be high, but even if it's a third of that amount, there's still a lot of inner traffic swirling around your brain, vying for attention.

What's really crazy is that 98 percent of the thoughts you have are the same ones you had yesterday. And up to 70 percent of those thoughts are negative. Now that calls for getting your mind right immediately!

What about you? Do thoughts like these crowd into your consciousness?

- *I'm in terrible shape and need to lose fifty pounds.*
- *I don't have enough education and don't think I'm qualified for the job.*
- *I don't have enough money, so I can't take the steps necessary to achieve the success I desire.*
- *I'll always be single.*
- *I just don't know if I can do it.*
- *They are a better team than us. I just don't think we can win this game.*
- *Why do I always mess up and sabotage myself? I'm horrible.*
- *I'm not good enough.*
- *I'm not any different than the millions of other people in the world.*

We can be cruel to ourselves and beat ourselves up with our thoughts and self-talk. This MUST stop.

The Bible talks about "taking every thought captive" in 2 Corinthians 10:5 (NASB), which, to me, means accepting responsibility for what you're thinking. You do have the ability to exercise control over your thoughts. How? You begin by realizing that you can think through your issues or problems rather than just reacting to them. You have the ability to deal with thoughts born of worry, fear, doubt, and even lust. That's what "taking every thought captive" is all about.

I'm well aware that everyone has negative thoughts every now and then. I include myself in that camp, but I try not to live in a dish of negativity. That's not going to get me where I want to go.

When I hear negative self-talk in my head—*Todd, you're too busy and have too much on your plate* or *Dude, who wants to listen to you? They've already heard this speech*—I'll reach for a three-quarter-inch-wide black band on my left wrist, pull it away from my wrist in a stretch, and let the band go.

Snap!

The stiff rubber is imprinted with yellow block lettering that says "I.M.P.A.C.T.," which stands for "live Inspired, Master your craft, Play at world class, take Action, Condition for greatness, and be Tenacious." When the IMPACT band snaps, it actually hurts a little. I don't do this for masochistic reasons; I do it to remind myself to cut off any negativity—or anything else I shouldn't be thinking about—immediately, before my own thoughts gang up and overwhelm me.

Experience has taught me that speaking about negative outcomes creates self-fulfilling prophecies. When you say things like *You're such a loser* out loud, you're turning your thoughts into words. Once words are said, an entire set of domino tiles starts falling, one after another. Here's what I love telling people:

Your thoughts become your words.

Your words become your flesh.

Your flesh becomes your actions.

Your actions become your habits.

Your habits become your character.

And your character becomes your legacy.

Everything begins with your thoughts, so let's take inventory. Are you constantly down on yourself or belittling your actions? Do you often feel like something bad will happen to you? Do you think you're unattractive, unloved, and unwanted?

Get in the habit of speaking positively to and about yourself. Maybe I do this because I get tired of snapping my IMPACT band, but I feel like I've gotten a lot better in this area. When I remind myself that I'm on the right track, that I'm succeeding at my endeavors to reach others with a message of positivity, then I'm even more inspired to make a difference in other people's lives. Positive self-talk is critical.

Some of my favorite sayings to myself are these:

- "We got this."
- "I want the pressure on my shoulders. Pressure is a privilege."
- "Come on, baby. Bring it on."
- "Oh, yeah. Wait until they see this."

In the sports world, we train athletes to visualize a successful outcome hundreds of times—like a dress rehearsal—before the competition starts. I've worked for a long time with Drew Brees, the quarterback of the New Orleans Saints. When Drew takes a seven-step drop and scans the field for a receiver to throw to, he sees—in his mind's eye—a perfect spiral leaving his fingertips and sailing through the air in slow motion before landing safely in the cradling arms of his receiver. He envisions nothing but positive outcomes for himself and for his team every time he drops back to throw the ball. Drew conditions his brain for success with every throw.

Another athlete I train, "Iron Mike" Chandler, is a mixed martial arts (MMA) champion and a former Bellator Lightweight World Champion. He's such a positive guy around the gym, working his butt off and giving high fives to everyone in sight. Mike embraces the "champion mindset" by creating a highlight reel of his best work inside the octagon and watching his winning moves over and over on a computer screen.

Chase Daniel, a quarterback with the Chicago Bears, asked the team videographer to prepare a three-minute video reel of all his completions in certain situations—first-and-ten; second-and-short; and third-and-long. Watching himself successfully make the throw every time left a great mental picture in his mind, assuring him that he belongs in the NFL.

Sure, sometimes quarterbacks throw an interception. Sometimes things don't go as planned in life. Sometimes we don't get the position we applied for, the promotion we hoped for, or the contract we expected. Every defeat hurts, but it doesn't have to define us.

I've heard Drew say many times that adversity equals opportunity. I've seen how adverse times were the prelude to something really good happening in my life. Even when reality didn't match my highlight reel, I got back up, dusted myself off, and got back to work.

THE POWER OF POSITIVE THINKING

Experience can be a great teacher, and comebacks start with forward motion in that space between your ears. This is the time to intentionally be thinking positively.

But how do you do that, Todd?

The short answer: pay attention to what you're doing the first hour after you wake up.

I already mentioned how I start my day with a "quiet time." You should consider doing the same, even if it's just fifteen minutes.

Reading inspirational literature or journaling positive thoughts before you start your day will boost your happiness and pave your road to success. There's nothing negative about that.

Reading has many advantages: you often learn something you don't know; you discover how to handle situations and people from others who have gone before you; you can be inspired by others' successes and insights; and you can envision a brighter future.

I try to read for thirty minutes every day. If I sink my teeth into a book, I can devour it in three days, but it usually takes me a couple of weeks to finish a book, especially if I'm only reading early in the morning or late at night.

Confession: I stop reading about half the books I start. If I'm thirty pages into a book and it's not holding my interest or I don't like the content, I stop right there and move on to the next book. (I sure hope you keep reading *Get Your Mind Right* after thirty pages!)

What types of books do I like to read? I prefer paging through books on personal development; autobiographies; how-tos on health, fitness, and performance; or business-related books.

I've been reading during my quiet time for the last twenty years and can assure you that making the effort to read has made a real difference in my life. It's the best way I know to learn new things and find inspiration. Reading slows life down and is also a welcome antidote to the fast-paced world that all of us tackle every day.

If you want to start your day with thinking good thoughts, then read a chapter or two from any book in the Bible plus a chapter from Proverbs. (There are thirty-one chapters filled with incredible wisdom, so you can read one a day for each day in a month with thirty-one days.) Get a devotional that's only one page long per day. Or choose something else that's uplifting and positive to read.

You'll be glad you did. Your thoughts will start to change, and that's the impetus for everything.

THE BENEFITS OF BREAKING A SWEAT

The second important thing you can do to start your day is to work out. I see this as imperative, not optional. I told Susan Fairgrieve this in the midst of her grief, and I tell my clients and athletes the same thing.

A great workout reduces negativity, dampens depression, wipes out pessimism, and decreases ill feelings because feel-good chemicals are released by the body during strenuous exercise. Powerful chemicals like dopamine, oxytocin, serotonin, and endorphins released during exercise supercharge both the body and the mind.

In addition, potent hormones like catecholamine, adrenaline, noradrenaline, hydrocortisone, and glucocorticoid interact with receptors in your brain, causing the immune cells to go crazy and flood the cardiovascular system. These hormones help protect the body against illness and can also relieve aches and pains. Exercise helps you feel good about yourself, builds self-confidence, and assists in warding off stress. Movement is *not* optional—it's mandatory if you want to get your mind right.

Another great thing you can do *while* working out is to listen to positive music or podcasts that can help you get your mind right. When you listen to music you enjoy, your brain releases large amounts of dopamine, a "feel good" neurotransmitter that causes you to feel emotions like happiness and joy.

Music is an incredible resource when it comes to getting your mind right. When I'm in the car, sitting in a plane seat, hanging out in a hotel room, or working out in my gym, I'll put on my Under Armour headphones and listen to some of my favorite tracks in the background. I also love listening to podcasts featuring people I admire like pastors Joel Osteen, Rick Warren, and T. D. Jakes, as well as leadership experts John Maxwell, Dave Ramsey, and Jon Gordon. I've also been known to indulge in personal growth

LAY OFF THE GOSSIP

We have another ironclad rule at Fitness Quest 10: no gossiping. In staff meetings, I've told my trainers and associates that I don't want anyone gossiping about a teammate, a client, or a club member. I put the no-gossip policy in place because we uphold positivity within our walls. If someone is gossiping *to* you, it won't be long before he or she is gossiping *about* you.

I also remind everyone at Fitness Quest 10 that if you listen to gossip and don't cut off the conversation, then you're just as much a gossip as the person spreading the stories. I think people like to gossip because it makes them feel better about themselves when they're cutting other people down. There's nothing positive about spreading hearsay and innuendo.

I despise gossip, and I'd tell anyone in a leadership position to nip it in the bud whenever they hear it, right when it happens. Speaking ill of others and gossiping about people is cancerous—and cancer will kill an organization or business.

junkies like Tony Robbins, Robin Sharma, Shanda Sumpter, and Marie Forleo.*

I have workout songs and chill-out songs. If I'm working out and need some energy in my music, then I'm listening to the *Rocky IV* soundtrack, songs from AC/DC or Metallica, NF's "Motivate" or "The Elements," "Baba O'Riley" from the Who, or "Lose Yourself" from Eminem. If I'm in a chill-out mood, then I have Fleetwood Mac, the Fray, Chris Tomlin, and Eric Clapton songs on my playlist. If I'm really getting at it in the gym, I've been known to put the same workout song on repeat for an hour-long session.

At Fitness Quest 10, we play energetic music in the background since chill-out songs don't quite cut the mustard. We also have a

*If you like, you can tune in to my podcast to help you further get your mind right: *The Todd Durkin IMPACT Show*. Check it out on iTunes, Stitcher, Spotify, or Google Play.

couple of large-screen TVs in our studio, but you're never going to see any of the news channels (CNN, MSNBC, and Fox News) on the air. That type of programming riles up people's emotions, often in a negative way. I don't know how you can be effectively swinging kettlebells and lifting weights while watching today's horrific news. If you're doing a stair-stepping or elliptical machine or running on a treadmill with a personal TV on your machine, be careful what channel you're watching. That's one surefire way to get your mind *wrong*!

TAKING A SWING AT LIFE

Let me finish with a story about a young man named Justin Markell. He was on the JV baseball team at his school and really struggling at the plate. One afternoon, Justin asked if he could talk to me in my office.

I know it takes a lot of guts to request a meeting like he did. My office is right off the gym floor at Fitness Quest 10, so it's not like no one would notice him walking into my workspace. But I'm glad he did ask me because I love working with teenagers on getting their minds right and thinking the right way.

Justin sat down, took a deep breath, and mumbled, "I'm in such a deep slump." Then the tears welled up as he began to share his inner thoughts.

"I can't get out of my head," he said. "When it's my at-bat, my knees are shaking and all I can think about is that I'm gonna strike out. I feel anxious and uptight. I can't swing the bat like I want to. Once I get a strike called on me, I'm sure I'm going to strike out—and then I do. What can I do about it? Can you help me?"

I talked to him about creating a positive highlight reel for himself, going all the way back to Little League. I asked him to visualize the doubles, triples, and home runs he'd hit in his days of youth baseball. Then we came up with mantras that he could repeat to himself when he stepped into the batter's box so that he wouldn't feel his knees shaking.

The mantra that Justin loved was this: *Rip it, rip it, rip it.*

Regardless of the count, the situation, or the score, his mantra was "Rip it."

What a change in his way of thinking! And what different results he experienced on his JV team. He started dominating at the plate, spraying the ball over the ballpark. I loved the texts he sent me after games, telling me how he'd done and what was working at the plate. Each text ended with this hashtag: #WeGotThis. Justin actually got pulled up to the varsity later in the season because of his success. His mindset shift led to his strong results.

When the season was over, he asked to see me again. This time when I escorted him into my office, he took out a small box from his backpack.

"Here, this is for you," he said. I unwrapped the gift and saw a glass case with a baseball inside.

I looked at the shiny white ball. He had autographed it and added this line:

Rip it #WeGotThis

It doesn't matter if you are sixteen years old like Justin, twenty-six, forty-six, or eighty-six, the positive thoughts you grab hold of will always make you a winner. Life will always be a battle between the ears, but if you get your mind right, you can go out and perform at your best.

Everything counts. What you watch. What you listen to. Who you hang out with. The self-talk you give yourself every single day. Every. Single. Thing. Counts.

So let me go through this one more time:

Everything begins with the way you think because your thoughts become your words, your words become your flesh, your flesh becomes your actions, your actions become your habits, your habits become your character, and your character ultimately becomes your legacy.

Remember this list. When you do, your mind will be right like never before!

KEY #3

Life Requires You to Overcome Obstacles

Success is not to be measured by the position someone has reached in life, but the obstacles he has
overcome while trying to succeed.

—Booker T. Washington, author and adviser
to presidents of the United States

In the summer of 2012, my world was rocked.

It was the morning of June 26, a Tuesday. I received a phone call from David Godfrey, a friend of mine. "Did you hear the news?" he asked.

Uh-oh. "What news?"

"Saw Man got hit by a car this morning while riding his scooter. He didn't make it."

"What do you mean he didn't make it?"

"Saw Man died."

I was too stunned to say anything. After a long pause, all I could manage was a scream: "Nooooo!"

Ken "Saw Man" Sawyer was my best friend and one of my first clients after I moved from Malibu to San Diego in 1997. And now he was gone. I couldn't imagine life without him.

Saw Man was a colorful character in his early fifties who would never be content to sit on a couch. Gregarious, fun, and explosively positive, he trained with me more for the camaraderie than the six-pack abs.

I first met him after I worked out a deal with the Hilton San Diego Resort & Spa on Mission Bay to offer a series of "boot camps" on their grounds. He and five other guys—who jokingly called themselves the "Stud Club"—met me every Wednesday morning at 6:30 to get their butts whipped into shape with weights and strength training.

When we met, Ken was in his late thirties, married with a couple of young kids, and fighting an extra twenty pounds around his midsection. He loved being pushed to his physical limits and hearing me bark at him, "GET YOUR MIND RIGHT!" He even returned for more punishment on Saturday mornings: a different boot camp class that involved more running, calisthenics, and competitive games like boot camp football and blob tag.

Ken never missed a workout. Rain, mud, hail, or a Santa Ana heat wave, he was there every Wednesday and Saturday morning. We became best friends, and Ken became my biggest cheerleader. I loved the guy. He was a pitch-perfect sounding board, someone I could trust with my dreams, my fears, and my future.

One time, I told Ken that I had greater plans than doing boot camps the rest of my life, which is why I was enrolled in graduate school at San Diego State. I explained that I could see myself being a kinesiology professor, but I wasn't sure if I wanted to go into the world of academia.

"Or maybe I'll open my own fitness studio," I ventured. "A place where I could motivate others to be the best they can be. I really want to make a difference in people's lives."

Saw Man nodded. "You should do that, TD. You'd be great at it. I can see you succeeding in every way possible. Just think—*Todd Durkin, fitness studio owner.* I like what I'm hearing."

I took those encouraging words to heart.

In the summer of 1999, shortly after I crossed the Coronado Bridge with Melanie and told her that I was turning down the professorship at College of the Canyons, I started thinking more seriously about opening a fitness studio where I could do personal training and massage therapy.

I was living in Mission Hills, a nice neighborhood near downtown San Diego that overlooked Lindbergh Field. I noticed that a six-hundred-square-foot commercial space a few blocks away was available. I asked for a tour. A twenty-by-thirty-foot studio wouldn't give me or my clients much room to maneuver, but it was all I could afford.

I would be emptying my bank account to lease such a small space.

One Saturday morning after a vigorous game of boot camp football on the sands of Mission Bay, I told Ken about the commercial space I'd seen in Mission Hills.

"How big is it?" he asked.

"Six hundred square feet."

I could see the objections written on his face. "Are you kidding me? You're *not* taking that space. You can *do better* than a six-hundred-square-foot broom closet. You'll outgrow that place in the first month."

"But if I get anything bigger, I can lose everything I have," I protested.

Ken stopped me there. "Lose everything you have? And what would that be? That crappy, beat-up old Volvo you're driving?"

He had me there. I was a twenty-eight-year-old bachelor sharing a cheap house rental with two roommates. My only tangible asset was a twelve-year-old Volvo 740 GLE four-door sedan with ripped velour hanging from the ceiling. The dented vehicle had 120,000 miles on the odometer and couldn't have been worth more than a thousand bucks.

Saw Man wasn't finished. "If you're going to do this, you need to look for a bigger place. Heck, you have nothing to lose. You barely have enough money to put gas into that piece of crap you're driving."

I smiled. I liked it when people spoke truth to me.

I didn't take the space.

OUT IN THE BOONIES

A couple of months later, one of my grad school professors shared an opportunity to work at a health fair in the San Diego suburb of Scripps Ranch. She said I could include this as part of my thesis work on the physiological and psychological effects of massage therapy on stress and anxiety.

Scripps Ranch? That was way out in the boonies, as far as I was concerned. Located about twenty minutes northwest of Mission Hills, Scripps Ranch was a few miles past Naval Air Station Miramar, where the Top Gun pilots trained. On the drive there, I noticed a lot of sagebrush to the east of Interstate 15. When I turned off the freeway, though, Scripps Ranch looked to be a nice community set in zillions of eucalyptus trees.

I did chair massage therapy at the health fair for anyone who visited our booth. When I was packing up, a middle-aged woman approached me. "Do you know of any Pilates, yoga, or training studios in this area?" she asked.

I chuckled. "Ma'am, I'm sorry, but I barely have any idea of where I am right now, let alone know where you'd find a Pilates or training studio, or a place to do yoga."

But a light bulb went off in my head. How could this nice area not have a Pilates, yoga, or training studio?

When the health fair was over, I drove around the leafy neighborhoods of Scripps Ranch. I got lost and stumbled upon a strip mall, where I pulled into the parking lot and noticed a vacant space on the second floor. There was a For Lease sign on the window.

I was up for an adventure. I parked and walked upstairs and looked into the empty retail space. The sign said that 2,000 square feet was available for lease and included a phone number to call.

I paused. Why would I open a fitness studio out here in the middle of nowhere?

I started walking away, but then I stopped in my tracks, turned around, and took another look. What I saw was a vision of my future.

Ever since I had checked out that six-hundred-square-foot place in Mission Hills, I'd been more and more consumed with the idea of opening my own fitness studio with personal training, Pilates, massage therapy, and yoga under one roof. I strongly believed I could help others looking to regain or improve their health. I had the personal experience of overcoming a serious back injury, and I'd spent the past five years with some of the best mentors and gurus in the state.

I wrote down the phone number since I didn't have a cell phone in 1999. When I got home, I called the leasing agent and described my idea about opening a training studio. He had no idea what I was talking about. Training studios really didn't exist in the late '90s.

"So you're like a physical therapist?" he asked.

"Kind of. I'm a physical trainer who also does massage therapy. I want to open up a studio where people can come train with me one-on-one and receive massage therapy, yoga, and Pilates."

Three months later, in January 2000, I was open for business in Scripps Ranch. Thank goodness I negotiated a lease that gave me the first three months for free, because I had no clients, save for a handful of people who saw me for massage therapy. I called my new place Fitness Quest 10.

The number 10 in the name refers to the way we rate things on a scale of 1 to 10, 10 being the best—and I wanted my fitness facility to be the best. Plus, 10 was also my jersey number growing up; I wore a 10 in every sport I played. Being the youngest of eight kids, along with Mom and Dad, made for 10 people in our family. Coincidentally, my wife's birthday is on the tenth of the month, along with two of my three kids. It's fair to say that 10 is my special number.

It's also fair to say that Fitness Quest 10 would have stayed a dream if it hadn't been for Saw Man. I kept thinking about this when I eulogized Ken at his memorial service following the tragic and senseless accident. A car making an illegal U-turn nailed Saw Man while he was riding his motorized scooter to meet a friend for an early-morning run.

"Ken was the guy cheering me on when I started doing big workout sessions in hotel ballrooms with hundreds in attendance," I said. "He'd tell me, 'Way to go, TD. Pack 'em in and start smelling up the place.'"

The pain and anguish of losing him was so deep. Following his memorial service, I wept for days and weeks, knowing that I'd never see his bright smile or hear his trash talk again. How could I overcome this loss? I missed him horribly and couldn't shake off the low feelings that remained. Where would I be if I hadn't followed through on Saw Man's advice to lease a larger commercial space?

If Fitness Quest 10 had never opened, I never would have trained NFL athletes like LaDainian Tomlinson, Drew Brees, or Darren Sproles, never would have authored three books, never would have spoken before thousands of people at various corporate events around the world, never would have appeared on an NBC reality show, and never would have become a leader in an industry I care very much about.

WE'RE ALL ON A JOURNEY

We're all on a journey. No matter what setbacks come your way, don't use them as an excuse to take your eye off the ball or your mind off the challenges ahead. That's what I had to learn from a young age. I'm not sharing my story to impress you but rather to impress *upon* you that we all have to overcome something in life.

I was raised in a broken home. My parents, Paul and Mary Durkin, got divorced when I was five years old. Throughout my elementary school years—a dramatic time in a child's physical, intellectual, emotional, and social development—my father was not in the picture.

We were supposed to be the all-American family. My parents met in high school at Our Lady of the Valley in Orange, New Jersey, in the late 1940s. They started dating their junior year in 1950. Upon graduation, my father started working at a manufacturing firm in Long Island, New York, while my mother went to nursing school.

They got married in 1955, when both of them were twenty-two. In those days, Irish-Catholic couples were expected to have large families, so my parents didn't waste any time. Two boys, Stephen and Paul, arrived first, followed by *five* sisters—Patti, Pam, Mary Beth, Judy, and Karen—and then me. If you're keeping score at home, that adds up to eight children over a fifteen-year period.

Dad settled the growing family in Brick Township, farther south on the Jersey Shore where housing prices were cheaper because of the distance to New York City. My father had a two-hour commute to Long Island, where he was the plant manager for a manufacturing company that produced incandescent light bulbs, heating elements, and windshield wiper blades. His 170-mile round-trip commute meant that he left the house at 6:00 AM and often didn't get home until 8:00 PM. I didn't see him very much during my preschool years.

When he was home, Mom's frustrations with raising, feeding, and caring for eight kids, basically as a single parent, spilled over into their marriage. They argued frequently and reached a point where they couldn't live under the same roof. After they divorced, Dad moved to Colorado for a new job opportunity in Denver.

Dad's absence left a gaping hole, which I felt acutely at home and at school. But there was another dynamic that shaped me, and it was being the last born in a large family—the "runt of the litter," as I constantly heard myself called. Sure, child psychologists will tell you that last-born children are social, outgoing, spontaneous, and high on people skills. But we also wear hand-me-down clothes and get picked on.

I had to fight for my place on the playground and deal with the embarrassment of being one of those "lunch ticket" kids who stood in a special line inside the school cafeteria and received a tray of food with a carton of milk because our family qualified for public assistance. When I looked around at my classmates, I saw newer shoes and clothes that didn't look like they had been washed a couple hundred times.

I was the kid who constantly got into fights. They called me "Tough Todd" because I'd go down to the bus stop after school, looking for a fight. When taunting words or dirty looks were exchanged, I charged ahead with my fists. I believe there was suppressed anger inside of me from five to ten years of age.

But that all changed when Dad came back. I was in the fourth grade when my father moved back to Brick Township to reconnect with his family. I got a lot of his time since my older brothers and sisters were either in college or starting their own careers.

Sacred Heart Church in nearby Bay Head had a Saturday evening Mass at 5:00 PM. Dad would pick me up and take me to church, which was a great bonding time for us. The rest of the week he was in the grandstands or standing on the sidelines watching and cheering me on during my practices and games. I was an athletic kid who played football in the fall, basketball in winter, and baseball in the spring. With his words of encouragement ringing in my ears, I shined when the official blew the starting whistle or the ump yelled, "Play ball!" Being one of the best athletes on the field or the gym floor lifted my self-esteem.

By the time I was thirteen, I had high school sports on my radar. I figured out that if I was going to get anywhere in life, then I had to find my own path to get there. From an eighth-grader's perspective, that meant playing quarterback at Brick Township High School and being coached by the venerable Warren Wolf, a legendary presence in New Jersey state football circles. If I played great and passed well, I could potentially earn a scholarship to play college football and get my tuition paid.

And that's what happened. I won a scholarship and played quarterback at The College of William & Mary, a Division 1-AA school, captaining the team my senior year. More importantly, though, I got a great education. I was a kinesiology major, which opened the door to what I do now—training professional athletes, inspiring fitness studio owners and managers, delivering keynote speeches at corporate events and business symposiums, and presenting internationally at fitness conferences and events.

One of the best things about my college years was receiving a handwritten letter *every single day* (except for Sundays, of course) from my father. His letters contained a quick note with a line or two of encouragement—"Keep working hard during the off-season because you'll be glad you did"—as well as newsy articles he clipped from our hometown newspaper, the *Asbury Park Press*.

And then one of the most difficult times of my life struck like a thunderbolt. On February 18, 1992, my sister Karen called to tell me that Dad had suffered a severe heart attack, and it looked like he had only a few days left. I flew home from Virginia to New Jersey that day and rushed to the hospital, where I got to see him and pray with him one last time. My father passed away early the next morning, February 19, 1992. He was only fifty-eight years old.

His passing paralyzed me. Everything was going pretty smooth in my life up until then, but if there was one person I didn't want to lose at that point of my life, it was my father, who was an incredible mentor to me. I couldn't believe he was gone or that I would never receive another letter from him.

The impact of his absence was immediate and profound. I'll admit that I was down and depressed. His passing took away all of my mojo, all of my confidence, and, quite frankly, all of my faith. I never questioned my belief in God before then, but in the days and weeks following his death, I did.

Following the funeral, I stayed home and took long drives to places we visited together, like the Great Auditorium in Ocean Grove and the inlet at Point Pleasant. I'd sit in my car and imagine him next to me, speaking words of wisdom. Then I'd start to cry.

The tears continued for several weeks. I couldn't shake the feeling that I'd never feel the same way about life without my dad by my side.

Three weeks after his death, though, I heard his voice in my heart. He said to me, *It's time to dust yourself off and get back to school. I will be there with you.*

I was sure he was speaking to me.

What Dad was telling me was that there was a time for grieving, and a time for healing. Even though I hadn't fully grieved his loss or healed from the suddenness of losing him, it was time to start the process.

Back in Williamsburg, Virginia, after missing several weeks of school, I settled back into my dorm room and checked my mailbox on the first floor. Among the junk advertisements was a letter—from Dad! I looked at the postmark. The letter had been mailed the day before he suffered his heart attack.

It was like he was speaking from the grave:

Todd,

It doesn't matter what you do in life, as long as you are happy. Whether it be a teacher and coach. A doctor. A politician. An athlete. A businessman. Whatever you choose to do, do it with all your heart and might. Make a difference in people's lives and be happy.

Remember that life is very precious and TIME is the most important asset we all have. Be sure to use it wisely. I will always love you regardless of what you do. It's who you become and the impact you create that's most important.

> Love,
> Dad

Those words filled my sails during my twenties. I eventually turned back to God, but even all these years later, the sudden death of my father is very much part of my story. He was my biggest cheerleader, my biggest fan, and my most impactful mentor. Not only did he make amends for not being there between the ages of five and ten, but he went above and beyond in the way he invested in me. He was full of encouraging words and pats on the back when we were together, and when we weren't, he took fifteen to twenty minutes a day to cut out news articles from the local newspaper and write a note that he dropped in the mailbox each afternoon.

What about you? If someone asked you to share your story today, what would you say? Are you finding your way or dealing with the curveballs that life throws you? Are you expecting the unexpected to happen? There will always be unforeseen and unpredicted events coming at you.

I've found that many people harbor doubt in their abilities and what they are capable of—I call these *limited beliefs*. This negative mindset holds them back from being who they ultimately can become.

I certainly dealt with limited beliefs as I was coming of age. When Dad left us, Mom worked her tail off to keep us in the same house with enough to eat and clothes to wear. She was a private duty nurse who worked odd shifts so she could be there when we got home from school and cook a wonderful dinner. Somehow, the good Lord always provided for us. I don't know how Mom did it, but she was the toughest and most loving woman. She was a survivor.

But we were part of the "working poor," which left me with a chip on my shoulder and took many years for me to overcome.

(There are times when that chip is still there, and those are times when I need it.) Nonetheless, thanks to mentors like my father, my high school football coach Warren Wolf, business coach Wayne Cotton, my wife, Melanie, and renewal in my faith, I've been able to work through the adversities and challenges in my life.

Is there anything you have to get past? If so, what's holding you back? What can you do to move forward?

I've found that being able to discuss probing questions like these with someone you trust—your spouse, a close friend, or someone you view as a mentor—can make all the difference. In fact, we all need an inner circle we can confide in and count on. Do you have a Saw Man (or Saw Woman) in your life?

I shudder to think what my life would be like without confidants like Ken Sawyer, so take the time to invest in others. When you do, you'll find that they'll invest in you too.

THE PATH TO SUCCESS

So what are some ways to move forward in life, some ways to deter your own limited beliefs? Here are some ideas to consider:

• **Treat others as you would want to be treated.** Yes, this is the Golden Rule, and you've probably heard it before. When you treat others with respect, compassion, and empathy—and they can see that in you—then you're living a life worth telling a story about. When you act like a jerk or say mean, biting words, however, people will remember how you conducted yourself with them. Instead, start with being a good listener. Yes, it takes effort to hear what someone is trying to communicate to you, but wouldn't you want that person to listen to what you have to say?

• **When it comes to being a good listener, be willing to listen to other voices.** I shudder to think where my life would be if I had blown off Saw Man or felt that he should mind his own business. I could have said to him, "I got this," but instead I brought him into my decision-making process. After listening to me, he pointed out something hidden in plain sight: a six-hundred-square-foot facility would be way too small for the dreams I harbored to change people's lives through becoming fit and healthy.

• **Dream big and then reverse engineer your success.** Speaking of dreaming big, which I talked about in chapter 1, let me remind you what actor Christopher Reeve said before his death: "So many of our dreams at first seem impossible, then they seem improbable, and then, when we summon the will, they soon become inevitable."

Notice the phrase *summon the will*. This means you have to get your mind right before you can do anything else. Are you waiting for opportunity or good fortune to drop in your lap? Or are you figuring out what you need to do to take the first step? Remember, the goal each day is to get 1 percent better or 1 percent closer to your goal. I preach this mantra every day in my gym.

When I say "reverse engineering," I'm referring to the process in which people take an object apart to see how it works in order to duplicate that object. When you dream big, you have to figure out what small goals will help you get there. Once that happens, you can start taking small steps in the right direction. The first step toward reaching one of your big goals might be signing up for a seminar, reading a book, or listening to a podcast.

Take that first step today.

• **Create a roadmap.** In 2005, five years after I opened Fitness Quest 10 but seven years before I lost Saw Man, I decided to make out an Intention Card, using one of those four-by-six index cards. What I did was write down seven intentions in my life, choosing seven because it's the number of completeness and perfection in the Bible.

I felt prompted by God's Spirit to share my thoughts for the future on this Intention Card because I found myself standing at one of those crossroads in life. We had outgrown our already expanded 3,000-square-foot space at Fitness Quest 10 and needed to expand—again. Saw Man loved teasing me about that.

But taking over another space to expand to 5,000 square feet would add another $10,000 a month to my costs. How was I going to cover that?

On my index card, I wrote down seven intentions or possible ways to make that happen:

1. Sell ten executive memberships at $1,000 a month where I personally coach and train these people on their health and life performance.
2. Start a Mastermind group for fitness pros who want more success.
3. Seek out a sponsorship by a major apparel company.
4. Start a membership plan at the gym. (We were scheduling only one-on-one sessions with a personal trainer at the time.)
5. Increase retail sales to $1,000 a month.
6. Make a seven-set DVD series on sports performance training.
7. Book five speaking engagements.

I carried my Intention Card everywhere. I saw progress in nearly all the items, but then something special happened with the third item—my desire for Fitness Quest 10 to be sponsored by a major apparel company.

First, I had no contacts at any company of that kind, so I didn't know where to start. Then, in the fall of 2006, Drew Brees had a great comeback from major shoulder surgery. He was training with me at the time. Drew guided the Saints to a 10–6 season record, which qualified New Orleans for the playoffs for the first time in a half-dozen years. He was also named to his second Pro Bowl, which was the annual NFL All-Star game played at that time after the Super Bowl in early February in Honolulu. As a thank-you for helping him revive his NFL career, Drew gave Melanie and me a trip to Hawaii to hang out with him and his wife, Brittany, in the warm sunshine.

One afternoon, I was standing on the sideline of the NFC All-Pro team's practice watching Drew and the Pro Bowl players run through drills when I overheard a conversation between two guys. One guy was talking about Under Armour, the company he worked for. I had heard of them—they were an up-and-coming sports apparel company known for producing moisture-wicking T-shirts made from microfibers. I hadn't forgotten that one of my intentions was to hook up with a major apparel company.

When he was free, I introduced myself to Bill Hampton, who was one of the right-hand guys of Kevin Plank, the founder and CEO of Under Armour. Back in the mid-1990s, when Plank was a fullback and special-teams standout at the University of Maryland, he hated how cotton T-shirts under his shoulder pads became soaked with sweat during practice and games. When he graduated, Kevin decided to make moisture-wicking shirts with a synthetic material. He called the company Under Armour and started selling apparel out of the trunk of his car. By 2006, Under Armour was really coming on in the sports apparel world.

Under bright Hawaiian sunshine, I blurted to Bill, "I have a vision to help change the world. Can we meet some time?"

The Under Armour executive was game. "Absolutely. How about eight o'clock tomorrow morning for breakfast?" he asked.

I stayed up all night in our hotel room writing out a detailed plan on how I could change the world, starting with Fitness Quest 10. Bill liked what he saw and showed my plan to Kevin Plank. Within a few months, we became the first training facility to be associated with Under Armour.

The sponsorship deal would have never happened if I didn't make it an intention, which is why roadmaps are so important. As Yankee great Yogi Berra said one time, "You've got to be very careful if you don't know where you are going because you might not get there."

• **Be willing to delay gratification.** They say it takes years to become an overnight success. From Thomas Edison to Henry Ford to Steve Jobs to Kevin Plank, to female entrepreneurs like Sara Blakely, founder of Spanx, and Cher Wang, whose HTC smartphones account for 30 percent of the global market, success was a mixture of hard work, perseverance, study, and sacrifice until they reaped the rewards.

When Fitness Quest 10 opened, it wasn't like I was flooded with people. It took time to build up a clientele, especially of professional athletes, and many years to branch out into speaking, being an author, and moving into the corporate world as a keynote speaker.

And there's always more to learn, no matter how much success you might experience. These days, I'm finding there's a new learning curve when it comes to producing content for social media—Instagram, Facebook, YouTube, and podcasting. I'm fine with that because I know I'm in this for the long haul.

• **Don't forget that life is a risk.** No matter what you do, you can't play it safe in life. Yes, prudence is important, but life has always involved a certain amount of risk, so you have to be willing to take chances after you've done your due diligence. That said, I go through self-reflection and prayer after I've collected the information I need to make an informed decision, asking God to lead the way if this resolution is part of His plan for my life.

For years, I relied on my own strength to make things happen, but that got tiring. Once I started reading the Bible regularly, focusing on Him in my quiet time, and leaning on God during good times and bad times, I felt like I was taking the right path.

• **Finally, give to others when possible.** On October 29, 2012, massive Hurricane Sandy roared into the Jersey Shore, destroying more than 600,000 housing units in New Jersey and New York and inflicting $70 billion in damage. Over eight million people lost power.

Sandy made landfall at Atlantic City and packed a big punch that flooded seaside communities bordering the Atlantic Ocean, including my childhood hometown of Brick Township. Mansions and bungalows alike ended up as curbside woodpiles filled with sand and seawater.

I felt like I had to do something for my old neighborhood, so I established a 501(c)(3) foundation in the wake of Hurricane Sandy to raise money for college scholarships to help underprivileged, underserved student athletes like myself back when I was graduating from high school. I wanted to make sure our funding priorities were directed at those affected by the natural disaster as well as childhood obesity, and diseases such as cancer and cardiovascular issues. I call it the Durkin IMPACT Foundation.

In the last seven years, we've donated over $250,000 in scholarships and helped more than forty young men and women realize their dream of attending college. Being part of that effort lifts my soul and inspires me to help others overcome tragedies and hardships in their lives.

It's a given that we will face trials, obstacles, and setbacks along the way, but what I've found is that mental toughness, spiritual fortitude, and an indomitable spirit will keep you moving forward. Stay the course with whatever challenge you're facing, reminding yourself that getting 1 percent better each day will teach you that you have greater courage, a greater ability to cope with hurdles, greater perseverance, and even more creativity than you ever dreamed you had.

That's what I mean about overcoming obstacles. When you press ahead, your life can be changed forever for the better. Instead of just getting through another bad day, you can come out of those experiences with an entirely new outlook because your mind is right.

SECOND QUARTER

EXECUTION
OF KEY PLAYS

The keys to getting your mind right often require creating powerful habits, employing best practices, and establishing routines so you can master your time, energy, and focus. It takes tremendous discipline to execute your game plan. Here is how you do it.

Habits Will Make or Break You

Discipline is the bridge between goals and accomplishment.

—Jim Rohn, author and entrepreneur

At Fitness Quest 10, we call it "The 5 AM Club."

Each weekday morning before dawn, my general manager, Jeff Bristol, and sports performance coach, Jesse Dietrick, lead a group of male and female corporate managers, sales associates, tech jockeys, and sleepy-eyed high school students through an intense, high-level, sweat-inducing, one-hour workout. I've seen how hard these folks work. They really get after it at a time when 90 percent of the world around them—that's an educated guess, of course—is still under the covers, still sleeping.

There's no better way to get your mind right than waking up before daybreak and clanking some iron, stretching the muscles, elevating the heart rate, and changing the physiology of the body. I might be a little prejudiced in feeling that way, but research shows that when you exercise and train—especially first thing in the morning—you experience a significant hormonal response. I've long believed that a rush of endorphins, the chemicals naturally produced by the nervous system to relieve stress and dull pain, gives you the energy to be on task all day.

I salute those who come to Fitness Quest 10 at daybreak to be part of the 5 AM Club. They *can't* cancel a workout they've already completed. What I'm trying to say is that I've noticed through the years that if you don't work out before you get to work, there's a solid chance it might not happen. Things come up: a kid gets sick, a project goes wrong, traffic tie-ups double the evening commute time, and before you know it, the day has gotten away from you and something needs to be cut. That something is often exercise.

Early morning workouts in a gym—or a spirited walk or jog around the neighborhood for twenty, thirty, or forty minutes as the sun comes up—give you clarity of mind, greater focus on tasks, more energy, and quite frankly, more happiness.

As an insider to the routines of the world's top athletes, I feel confident in stating that great habits get your mind right. Here are a few ideas to keep in mind:

• **First, make a commitment, and when you do, stick to it.** So many of us go through life without committing to anything. We take life as it comes. Or we're too busy to do anything beyond the basics—get up, go to work, go home, and go to sleep. Exceptions might be hitting happy hour with the work crew or meeting friends at your favorite craft brewery on the weekends.

In order to have a better tomorrow, the first thing you have to do is make a commitment *today* to better yourself. This commitment is a key step in getting your mind right. After thirty years in the fitness field, I know firsthand that the road to the gym is paved with good intentions. Once people step inside the gym, though, they're glad they made the effort to get there, no matter the hour.

• **Be a thermostat, not a thermometer.** A thermometer has the single purpose of telling you the temperature of the environment.

If it's hot outside, the thermometer will tell you if it's in the 90s or triple-digit heat. If it's freezing, well, you'll know that as well, but that's the purpose of a thermometer—to *reflect* what's happening around you.

A thermostat, on the other hand, *regulates* the environment. When you set a thermostat to a certain temperature, the device signals the air conditioner or the heater to lower or raise the temperature in the room. It's you who decides how hot or how cold, and you can control the temperature.

You want to be a thermostat in life—constantly monitoring your surroundings and making adjustments. *Influence* your surroundings instead of letting them influence you. When you act like a thermostat, you set the temperature of your environment.

• **Be prepared to do things that people never see.** The members of the 5 AM Club are unsung heroes. There are no parades given to those who wake up to a 4:30 alarm, splash water on their faces, throw some clothes on, and head out the door to exercise at the appointed hour.

Success is rooted in unseen, uncelebrated sacrifices. But talk to those who get up early to exercise, and they will tell you that the results speak for themselves. They get their minds right because they decided they would do something to improve their lives and acted upon those commitments.

• **Know that hard work beats talent when talent doesn't work hard.** I mentioned earlier that I've been working with New Orleans Saints quarterback Drew Brees for the better part of sixteen years. Throughout this time, I have never seen Drew back off in the gym. He always said he wanted to be the hardest worker in the room, and he proves it every time he steps into Fitness Quest 10.

How much effort are you putting into your fitness? Are there times when you "take a rep off," as we say in the gym? Coasting will cost you in big and small ways. A lackadaisical effort means that you'll fall behind in your fitness and trail your contemporaries.

Go after it in the gym, and you'll always be the hardest worker in the room.

If you've never been pushed, sign up with a personal trainer or participate in a group exercise class to see what you're missing.

• **Become a person of routine.** The highest performers are typically men and women of routine. They know what they'll be doing today, tomorrow, and the rest of their foreseeable future—because they've planned for it. They are the ones who commit to a 5 AM Club, join a local cycle club for a Saturday morning ride, or book a trainer three times a week.

Having a routine is another way of saying that you've established certain customs or patterns of behavior, which are better known as habits. Everybody has habits, whether they're aware of them or not. If there are too many bad habits in your life—like skipping workouts, eating junk food, or staying up late to play video games—they will take over your life like weeds infesting a garden.

So let me ask you this: What are your habits like? Which ones take precedence in your life? The reason I ask is because many are unaware that they have fallen into a rut of bad habits. They get up each morning, shuffle into the kitchen, flip on the coffee maker, and start their morning shower. They sip their cup of joe while they dress, grab a bowl of cold cereal, and sprint through the front door to join the rat race. When the workday is over, they drive home, eat dinner (either at a fast-food restaurant or straight out of the microwave), check out social media with the TV going in the background, and fall asleep as *The Tonight Show* comes on.

I realize that these are generalizations, but ask yourself, do these habits look anything like yours? There's more to life if you can develop a new routine and get your mind right.

• **Remind yourself that it takes time to establish new habits.** It's often been said that it takes twenty-one days to form a new habit. I've been skeptical of that number because I've witnessed with my own eyes how long it takes people to *really* establish a new routine. It's considerably longer than twenty-one days.

The "twenty-one days to establish a new habit" maxim came from a blockbuster book written in the 1960s by Maxwell Maltz, a plastic surgeon who noticed that it took around three weeks for a patient to get used to seeing his or her new face. The book, *Psycho-Cybernetics*, sold thirty million copies and was highly influential, but many overlooked Dr. Maltz's main assertion, which was that it took a *minimum* of twenty-one days for an old mental image to dissolve and a new one to appear.

There are many voices that challenge Maltz's assertion. I listened to a podcast by leadership expert Robin Sharma, who said it takes sixty-six days to wire in a new ritual. I buy into the longer length of time. It's hard work creating champion habits. Three weeks isn't long enough.

That said, don't let me discourage you. Whether it's a few weeks or a couple of months, it really doesn't matter how long it takes you to establish good habits and a healthy lifestyle—what matters is that you do it. What matters is that you take the necessary steps to break out of your humdrum routine and start *new* habits that will help you get your mind right. Once your mind is renewed, you'll find change much easier to accomplish.

Let me give you some ideas on how you can ignite your mindset and catapult your results into all areas of your life.

AM ROUTINE

• **Beat the sun up.** Hear me out before you close this book or your Kindle app. What I'm talking about is establishing a sixty- to ninety-minute morning routine that involves a "quiet time," a workout, a shower, and a healthy breakfast before you start your day. If you have to leave the house at 6:30 AM, all cleaned up and ready to go, that means waking up at 5:00 AM. If you don't have to leave the house until 8:00 AM, then 6:30 AM is going to work.

If nothing else, get up before the sun comes up and spend fifteen minutes going for a walk, practicing yoga, or doing some breathing exercises. Your body and mind will thank you for your effort, and your energy will be awakened.

• **Don't turn on your phone right after you wake up.** I call the first sixty minutes of the day my "holy hour"—a time when I awaken my mind, move the body, and awaken my soul. My energy gets amped up as I prepare to dominate the day ahead. I want you to embrace the idea of a "holy hour."

If you check your smartphone before you complete your morning routine, there's a good chance you won't complete it at all. Before you know it, a half hour will fly by and you haven't completed one task or even warmed up your muscles. More importantly, you haven't gotten your mind right at all if you jump into answering emails, scrolling through your favorite news sites, and checking out how many likes you got for your latest Instagram posts. You're spinning your wheels when you put that smartphone in your hand or fire up your laptop after wiping the sleep from your eyes.

• **Start your day by taking ten to twenty minutes to nurture the soul.** I mentioned in my introduction how I spend a concentrated amount of time each morning reading the Bible and follow it with prayer and journaling before I do anything else—including exercise.

I get to know God and His will for my life by reading Scripture. I learn so much when I study my Bible: the history of the universe, what sin is, and how we have the assurance of eternal life when we believe in Jesus. Scripture also contains godly principles for living right as well as great wisdom, especially in the book of Proverbs. I don't know about you, but I need to hear that timeless wisdom every day, which is why I also read a chapter of Proverbs each morning.

And then I pray. Prayer is the way we communicate with God, but it's also an opportunity to praise Him for all He has done in our lives. Prayer is a time to share our feelings and what's happening in our lives, as well as an opportunity to cast our doubts and burdens at the feet of Jesus. I feel so much better starting off the day with prayer. It's like wiping the slate clean. Talk about getting the mind right!

Maybe the idea of prayer makes you feel totally lost. That's okay. There are some great models out there for prayer routines. I once heard Pastor Miles McPherson of the Rock Church in San Diego share the acronym AWCIPA as a model for prayer. Here's what the acronym stands for:

- A—admire and thank God
- W—wait quietly before God and listen
- C—confess your sins
- I—intercede for others
- P—petition for yourself
- A—admire and thank God again

That's a pretty good model to follow. Think about the order here: when you start your prayer time by admiring and thanking God, you're setting the right tone for the prayer that follows. Waiting quietly before God means that you recognize your position before God—He is Lord, and you are His child.

When you confess, you acknowledge that you are a sinner. This reality check keeps you right with God. When you pray for others, you are interceding on their behalf. After you've done these things, you can lift up your own needs. Then bring your prayer time full circle by finishing with an expression of your admiration for what God has done in your life as well as thanking Him for His tremendous blessings.

• **Journal to quiet your mind and establish your goals.** When my prayer time is over, I reach for my journal. I share my innermost thoughts, jot reminders, and sketch out future plans on the blank pages of a leather-bound journal. My reason for choosing an expensive journal: if the actual journal itself is special, then what I'm writing *inside* the journal is special as well.

You can certainly use a cheap spiral-bound notebook if you prefer. What's most important is that you take a few moments to summon your thoughts, record your memories, and express yourself on paper. When you open up your journal, spend time writing down what you sense the Lord saying to you as well as things that you are grateful for.

Journaling can help you clear your head, which gets your mind right, and create a repository of your thoughts and feelings. Sometimes seeing those thoughts and feelings on paper gives you clarity on what your next steps should be.

• **Shoot for twenty minutes.** I normally spend twenty minutes on this trifecta—reading my Bible, praying, and journaling—but if you're starting out, ten minutes will be just fine. Once you get into this new habit a few times, you'll be eager to go longer.

• **Meditation can work too.** When it comes to having a quiet time, some people prefer to meditate, which is fine. Prayer is *talking* to God and meditation is *listening* to God. If you prefer listening to God instead of beseeching Him in prayer, then go for it. And if you're not a person of faith, just sit and be still. There is tremendous power in silence and solitude. What's most important is tapping into your inner being early in the morning, which ignites your energy and spirit for the rest of the day.

• **When you're done nurturing your soul, get a move on.** After you've finished reading, praying, and journaling for ten to twenty minutes, it's time to exercise for a minimum of thirty minutes.

What if you don't have a home gym like I do? Well, you probably have a floor. That's good enough for plenty of exercises. You can march in place for a minute or two to warm up, and then you can perform squats and lunges. You can execute push-ups or various yoga-like poses. You can use dumbbells, TRX suspension training equipment, or sport cords in powerful ways. You can follow a home exercise program on your computer or smartphone. You can read more about training in Key #6: Train to Win.

I think you're going to be better off, however—and more likely to stick with a consistent exercise program—by going to a nearby fitness facility, preferably one within fifteen minutes of where you live. (Proximity is important when it comes to choosing what gym to join.) If going back and forth to a gym adds another fifteen minutes to a morning program, that must be factored in.

• **Finish the "holy hour" with ten minutes of stretching and recovery exercises.** The practice of stretching after moderate or intense exercise is necessary to reduce muscle soreness, increase blood flow to certain areas of the body that need it, prevent injuries, and help your muscles recover. And the older you get, the more you need to stretch.

Who else needs more stretching? Get it in and you will feel better and move better!

• **Recover with a protein shake and a hot-and-cold shower.** Protein plays an important role in repairing your muscles after exercise because it contains amino acids needed to restore your body. Research has shown that the sooner you consume high-quality protein after a workout, the better.

On *Strong*, I introduced Devon Cassidy to whey protein shakes, which I agree can be an acquired taste. Many protein-shake options on the market contain artificial sweeteners like aspartame, sucralose, and saccharin and fail the taste test. Choose a protein shake with natural sweeteners like organic cane sugar and a pinch of Stevia.

After I down my protein shake, I contrast a hot-and-then-cold shower to reset, recalibrate, and rejuvenate my body. I realize that this practice may not go over with everybody, but you can change the temperature of the water until you find a "refreshing" temperature that you can stand. Cold- or cool-water showers boost circulation, speed up muscle soreness and recovery, ease stress levels, and it will certainly wake you up!

If you really want to up your shower game, perform Wim Hof breathing exercises while you're in there. You may be thinking, *Huh? What are those?* Wim Hof breathing exercises are named after a Dutch athlete in his sixties who has set all sorts of records for exposure to extreme cold. His astounding feats of cold endurance include running a half marathon above the Arctic Circle clad in shorts and bare feet and swimming among ice floes in freezing water. His nickname is "The Iceman."

Wim Hof developed a set of breathing exercises that involve thirty quick breaths, inhaling through your nose and exhaling through your mouth. (You can find videos and explanations galore with a quick Google search.) After completing those, take a deep breath and exhale, and then hold your breath until you need to breathe in. Complete three rounds of this breathing exercise.

I perform these Wim Hof exercises during my morning showers and highly recommend them.

• **Finally, eat a healthy breakfast.** I won't get into specifics here since I share my thoughts on eating healthy in Key #7, but let me state the obvious: munching on a bagel smeared with cream cheese while downing your coffee as you step out of the house will not give you the proper fuel you need for your day.

PM ROUTINE

• **Remember: success the next day starts with the night before.** If you're having trouble with a morning routine, it's probably because your nighttime routine isn't great. I believe a good night-time routine is imperative for getting your mind right the next day. Many people go to sleep with stressed-out minds and anxious thoughts bouncing around their heads, which impacts the quality of their sleep.

• **No caffeine after 2:00 PM.** Coffee or tea with caffeine—the "high-octane" stuff—has a significant effect on sleep disturbance. A study by researchers at the Sleep Disorders & Research Center at Henry Ford Hospital in Detroit found that consuming caffeine six hours or less before bedtime reduced total sleep time by one hour.

• **Go easy at the dinner table and refilling that wine glass.** Stuffing yourself with thirds and fourths or grabbing that extra dessert can impact the quality of your sleep as your digestive system struggles to do its job during the night. Your body isn't designed to digest heavy meals, and your kidneys become overtaxed when you drink an excessive amount of alcohol.

• **Do the "two-minute drill."** Before you go to bed, take a moment to review your journal. Was there something you wanted to do but didn't get to today? Do you have any last-minute thoughts to write down before you sleep?

• **Power down.** Just as it's not a good idea to look at your electronic devices when you wake up, you should turn off those same devices thirty minutes—one hour is better—before you go to bed. Answering emails, engaging in your social media accounts, and web browsing make it difficult to settle down and fall asleep because of the way electronics physiologically and psychologically stimulate you.

When I say "electronics," I'm referring to smartphones, laptops, tablets, and yes, even TV screens. According to the National Sleep Foundation, the use of electronic devices before bed delays your body's internal clock, suppresses the release of sleep-inducing melatonin, and makes it far more difficult to fall asleep once you turn off the lights and lay your head down on your pillow. Yet 90 percent of American adults admit to using a technological device during the hour before turning in.

The number is that high because watching TV before bedtime is as natural as brushing teeth for some people. Others feel that watching TV *helps* them fall asleep. While watching some mindless TV before going to bed might be okay for some, I'd stay away from violent movies, local news shows with the latest shootings, or political commentary shows that feature guests arguing with each other over the latest issues of the day. All that in-your-face contention raises everyone's blood pressure.

I recommend setting an "electronic curfew" thirty or even sixty minutes before you hit the sack and drawing a line to not answer email or read social media posts before your bedtime.

• **Read something inspirational.** Reading an old-fashioned book can be soothing. I prefer to read inspiring nonfiction that lifts my spirits. You can also use e-readers like the Kindle Paperwhite because these tablets have the right type of "e-ink" that's different than the blue light coming from a smartphone or iPad. They won't keep your brain buzzing the way that a smartphone will.

• **Take zinc and magnesium before you go to bed.** These nutrients have been shown to be involved in the brain processes that control sleep. Zinc supports your immune system and regulates sleep. Magnesium is a natural sedative that helps your muscles relax and reduces the levels of cortisol, a stress hormone.

Some people prefer melatonin, an over-the-counter supplement. Melatonin is a naturally occurring hormone that affects your sleep-wake cycle. Our bodies normally produce enough melatonin to feel drowsy, but if you're having a stressful work week or have changed time zones recently, then melatonin can help.

• **Use a meditation app.** Having trouble falling asleep? There's an app for that. Calm and Headspace are two of the leading meditation apps and exude a calm vibe to help you calm down and improve your mood.

Wait a minute, Todd. Don't you have to use your smartphone or tablet to access the apps?

You certainly do. I'm just saying that when all else fails, then maybe apps like Calm and Headspace can help you relax. I've used them and was surprised to find that these guided meditations are quite good.

• **Charge your smartphone in the kitchen.** It's remarkable how many people leave their smartphone on their nightstand. One Gallup poll showed that 63 percent of all Americans keep their smartphones within arm's reach—or even tucked underneath their pillows!

I understand that many use the alarm clock feature to wake them up in the morning, but you can buy a cheap alarm clock. Even if the smartphone is on "silent," there's still a distinct buzz every time you receive a text or email during the night. By leaving your smartphone outside the bedroom, you minimize disturbances to your sleep and temptations to check your smartphone during the night or first thing upon waking.

• **Set the right temperature.** For optimal sleep, the bedroom temperature should be 67 degrees. Your body temperature decreases as the night goes on, so if the bedroom is too warm, you could wake up or sleep fitfully. Plus, if it's too warm, you'll dehydrate your body even more than what naturally occurs while you sleep.

• **Pray before you say goodnight.** If you pray to start the day, then it makes sense to pray before you sleep. One of my "best practices" is reaching over to Melanie, clasping my hand over hers, and praying together before we go to sleep. This is one of the most powerful things we do as a couple and a reminder that our relationship is based on our mutual faith in Christ.

If you want to change your world and change your mind, then pray with your spouse. And if you are not of faith, just spend a few moments in gratitude for breath and the many gifts in life. An attitude of gratitude always shifts mentality in the right direction and will help you get a great night's rest.

• **Shoot for between seven and eight hours of sleep a night.** I work backward: since I want to get up at 5:00 AM, that means I better be asleep by 10:00 PM since I'm used to operating on seven hours of sleep. I prefer seven and a half hours, meaning a 9:30 PM start is better. For most healthy adults, seven hours is a minimum amount of sleep. You may find that you function at your best with eight hours. If so, adjust accordingly.

• **Cycle through your four REM cycles each night.** If you're a good sleeper, then you're passing through four stages of REM or rapid eye movement sleep. Of course, there's no way to know if you're cycling through all four REM cycles since you're supposed to be asleep, but there are devices like the Oura Ring that you wear on a finger to monitor a range of physiological measurements while you sleep. Another device called the Withings Aura Smart Sleep System is a combination smart alarm clock with advanced sleep tracking, as long as you buy the accompanying sleep sensor mattress pad. If you're curious about your sleep quality, you can invest in some of these tools.

• **Finally, don't hit the snooze button.** For some reason, I have the gift of waking up at 5:00 AM without an alarm clock. For those who don't, an alarm is called for. Don't be the type who sets the alarm thirty minutes before you *really* need to get up. Sleep between alarm soundings is not high-quality sleep because your REM sleep has been disrupted. Skip the snooze. Get up the first time you hear that alarm in the morning.

CREATE YOUR RULES FOR LIFE

One of the things I did five years ago was create "rules" for my life. When I abide by my rules and am dialed into them, life works best.

I started with five rules. Now I have thirteen.

What's important for you isn't what my rules are. What's important here is that you create your own rules and live by them. A good place to begin is by answering a few questions like these:

- What do you need to do to look, feel, or perform your best?
- Are there any things, people, or habits that you need to avoid or eliminate in your life because they don't allow you to be your best?

Before you start creating your rules, take a look at mine. Then you can start with five or ten rules. Be specific. You can always add more.

Remember: These are my 13 rules. I share them so you can see my best practices and what I'm aiming to achieve.

My 13 Rules for Getting My Mind Right

1. I will get at least seven hours of sleep each night, so I adjust my bedtime accordingly. I will also get two massages per month. Bodywork does amazing things.

2. I will avoid caffeine after 2:00 PM and drink no more than two beers or glasses of wine per month.

3. I will train for at least forty minutes first thing *every* morning. This includes a minimum of ten to twenty minutes of prayer time, followed by thirty minutes of movement. I will listen to an inspirational podcast while exercising.

4. I will not turn on the phone until I'm done with my morning routine. And that goes for checking email as well.

5. I will think about the power of one. Who will be the "one" person today that I'm going to channel energy to and pour love, encouragement, and motivation on?

6. I won't swear. I will use words and vocabulary that increase the positive vibe in a room.

7. I will do my best to make sure I win the day. I am in control with *how* I choose to spend my time, *whom* I spend it with, and *what* I spend my time doing.

8. I will write down my WLAGs every Sunday—my **Wins**, **Losses**, **Aha moments**, and my **Goals** for the upcoming week. I want to create my "Daily Big 5" for each day too.

9. I will write in my journal daily for at least five or ten minutes.

10. I will be positive in my interactions and communication with everyone I'm in contact with—be it in person, online, or through social media. I will avoid negative interactions in person or online.

11. I will share my desire to motivate, inspire, and create impact with 10 million people in the world. I can't wait!

12. I will live a life guided by purpose and passion. I will not be steered by jealousy, gossip, temptations, or energy vampires. I will let my big, hairy, and audacious goals motivate and inspire me to do my best work.

13. Finally, I understand that I cannot and will not please everyone. I will focus on living each and every day with zero guilt on how I

conducted myself, with what I said or did, the decisions I made, or my actions, knowing that I did my absolute best to be the best father, husband, coach, leader, and person I can possibly be.

And here's one more list I created for myself.

My "Do Not" List

1. I won't hit the snooze button.
2. I won't turn on the phone when I wake up.
3. I won't check my email first thing in the morning. Or check my email as the last thing at night.
4. I won't immediately answer every phone call or text that comes in at all hours of the day.
5. I won't mindlessly surf the internet while in bed—or when kids are present on weekends.
6. I won't consume food and drink that makes me feel tired and sluggish.
7. I won't waste time engaging in conversation and arguments about topics that I have no control over.
8. I won't have any screen time (phones, computer, TV) thirty minutes before bed.
9. I won't be guided by making decisions because of financial ramifications. I will be sure all decisions feel right in the gut, are aligned with my core values, and make business sense in terms of my corporate culture, team camaraderie, etc.
10. I will not neglect my family. I will prioritize time with *who* is in my life, not *what* is in my life.

A CLOSING THOUGHT

How about you? What are your rules? What are your best practices and habits? The best way to cement them in your mind is to write them down, post them on four-by-six cards, share them with close friends, and most importantly, *live them.*

Prior to his passing in 2019, Sean Stephenson, a wonderful motivational speaker who stood three feet tall, used a great acronym to discuss these things. Sean talked about having your "WLWL," which stands for "when life works list." In other words, when life was working best for you, what were you doing?

Who were you spending time with?

How were you living?

What habits were you doing or not doing?

What was your mindset?

Design your rules so that when you execute them, you engage in good habits. It's critical that you set strong winning habits that will create a championship mindset in you. Don't forget that everything that comes into the brain is processed and will either have a positive or negative energy effect on your body, mind, or spirit.

My hope is that your habits will foster strong routines in your life and manifest high-octane fuel to turbocharge your results.

And then your mind will really be on the right track.

KEY #5

Be a Master of Your Time, Energy, and Focus

> One reason so few of us achieve what we truly want is that we never direct our focus; we never concentrate our power. Most people dabble their way through life, never deciding to master anything in particular.
>
> —Tony Robbins, motivational speaker

If you've ever seen me speak or deliver a keynote address, then you know I'm not the wallflower type who stands behind a hotel podium dressed in a conservative business suit and somberly drones on and on from a prepared speech while half the audience drifts away.

Those who come to hear me speak are in for a totally different experience. Equipped with a wireless microphone and often dressed in an Under Armour collared shirt and casual khakis, I like to jump off the stage and get eye level with my audiences. Then I raise my energy about two notches and get a bit animated:

> Today, I'm fired up to be talking about high performance and what it takes to be successful in today's competitive landscape. Whether

you're a fitness enthusiast, weekend warrior, desk jockey, athlete, or someone who wants to get back into shape, I'm going to show you the skills, the best practices, the disciplines, and the routines necessary to tap into your full potential and reach maximum success. I'm going to talk about the grit, the grind, and the mindset necessary to get to an entirely new stratosphere in life. Does that fire you up? Good, because we're about to set this place on fiyaa!

My delivery is as fast as a New Jersey fast-talker, and my energy can awaken sleeping giants. People call me a "high energy" guy in typical circumstances. But when I'm onstage, with the lights up and the intensity meter sky-high, I bring out my best so I can bring out other people's best.

How does this deal with time, energy, and focus? In every single way! Energy is the most precious commodity we have. Time is our most important asset. And if you can't focus your time or energy, you can't accomplish what you truly desire in life. Time, energy, and focus all work together when it comes to getting your mind right.

Let's start with *time*. There never seems to be enough time in a day to do the things we need to do, let alone the things we want to do. Technology was supposed to save us gobs of time, make us more efficient, and power us through the day, but that utopian existence hasn't happened yet and never will. Our waking hours have been encroached upon—even taken over—by smartphones, computers, and social media apps.

There's nothing new in what I just said. The first person who declared, "There aren't enough hours in a day" probably roamed this earth when Noah and his sons were constructing the ark. But as world-renowned performance psychologist Dr. Jim Loehr noted, energy, not time, is our most precious resource, as well as a future indicator of high performance. Here's what he wrote in his bestselling book, *The Power of Full Engagement*:

> Most of us are just trying to do the best that we can. When demand exceeds our capacity, we begin to make expedient choices that get us

through our days and nights, but take a toll over time. We survive on too little sleep, wolf down fast foods on the run, fuel up with coffee and cool down with alcohol and sleeping pills. Faced with relentless demands at work, we become short-tempered and easily distracted. We return home from long days at work feeling exhausted and often experience our families not as a source of joy and renewal, but as one more demand in an already overburdened life.

What's interesting is that Dr. Loehr wrote these words in 2003, four years before Apple released the first iPhone and launched the smartphone revolution with a large touchscreen that allowed users to flip through websites and apps with ease. The problem Dr. Loehr captured was exacerbated, not alleviated, by the new tech. Since we can do just about anything on a smartphone—hunt for jobs, find a date, book airline tickets, take photos, make videos, read books, or watch movies—these technological wonders have a unique way of taking over our lives and keep us from focusing on what's really important.

Let's take stock of reality with a few questions:

- Do you know how many times a day the average person checks out his or her cell phone?

  Answer: Once every twelve minutes, or an average of eighty times a day, according to a national study by Asurion, a global tech company. Ten percent of people check their phones once every *four* minutes. One-third of the 2,000 respondents said they felt anxiety when separated from their phones for any length of time.

- Do you know what the average "screen time" is for adults each day?

  Answer: Eleven hours. That's how long American adults spend watching TV, viewing YouTube videos, perusing their favorite social media sites and apps, and catching up on their emails and text messages, according to the market-research group Nielsen. That's crazy! That's

109

nearly two-thirds of one's waking hours staring at a flat-screen TV, computer monitor, or smartphone.

- Do you think the average "screen time" for teens is longer or shorter?

  Answer: Shorter, but not by much. Teens spend an average of *nine* hours a day looking into their phones, according to research done by Common Sense Media. It's probably because they're in school for approximately six or seven hours a day and aren't allowed to be on their phones during class. Otherwise, it would be worse!

- Finally, do you know how much time the average worker is productive in an eight-hour day in the US?

  Answer: Research suggests that during an eight-hour day, the average worker is productive for only two hours and fifty-three minutes. That's right—less than three hours a day! What are they doing instead of working? Here's a list of the most unproductive activities:

  1. Reading news websites: 1 hour, 5 minutes

  2. Checking social media: 44 minutes

  3. Discussing non-work-related things with coworkers: 40 minutes

  4. Searching for new jobs: 26 minutes

  5. Taking smoke breaks: 23 minutes

  6. Making calls to partners or friends: 18 minutes

  7. Making hot drinks: 17 minutes

  8. Texting or instant messaging: 14 minutes

  9. Eating snacks: 8 minutes

  10. Making food in the office break room: 7 minutes

Reading this Top Ten list makes me cringe when I think of the time, energy, focus, productivity, and money lost in the workplace.

Do you know how long it takes to get refocused after someone drops by your office or workstation to chitchat? The answer is twenty-five minutes, according to Gloria Mark, a distraction expert at the University of California, Irvine. This doesn't mean you have to be rude the next time a colleague drops by your office or workstation to tell about their weekend ski trip, but a gentle "I really need to finish something up here" might get you back on task sooner and make you more productive. Every minute counts, especially to your employer.

Think about the times when you *are* engaged in a meaningful conversation—at work or in your personal life—and the person's smartphone buzzes.

Excuse me. Can I get that?

What can you say other than, "Sure, go ahead"? The next time it might be you receiving an important call or text from home, so of course you say it's no problem.

But if the other person jabbers away or gets into a texting frenzy, then you might feel disrespected and experience a loss of trust. The *Journal of Social and Personal Relationships* performed a study on how cell phone use affects trust by asking half the people in a control group to put their cell phones on the table and the other half to keep their cell phones in their pockets or purses. The group with the cell phones on the table felt there was less trust between them, but trust scores soared when the cell phones weren't visible.

It's human nature: people are more likely to engage in give-and-take conversation when they can maintain eye contact and not be interrupted by phone calls and texts. It would be nice if people remembered that, especially on the roads. Distracted driving— like texting with one hand and steering with the other—results in approximately nine deaths and a thousand injuries *every day*, according to the National Highway Traffic Safety Administration.

Listen up, folks: we live in an era of distractions, digital or not. The more accurate phrase would be that we live in an era of *addiction.* This phenomenon is killing our productivity as well as our ability to focus not only on the tasks at hand but on just about anything other than our smartphones.

We need to get our minds right about technology because it's clear that smartphones are sabotaging the brain's ability to focus. At work. At home. In relationships. And in our own health and well-being.

We *must* do something to use technology as a "tool" versus as a "weapon of destruction"—especially in the world of social media.

SOCIAL MEDIA OR SERVICE MEDIA?

Disclaimer: Let me start by saying that I love social media. I really do.

But when it comes to maximizing your time, energy, and focus, you have to be aware of social media and how it impacts your life. Many people, especially those between the ages of 12 and 30, are incredibly wrapped into what people are saying on Instagram, Facebook, Snapchat, Twitter, LinkedIn, and YouTube. They even determine their self-worth by how many likes they receive after posting their most recent selfie.

And what about the comments that people write in response? It can be a free-for-all out there, and one thing I've learned over the years about social media is that people can be ruthless. I'm talking about the comments filled with snark and sarcasm. It's best to ignore them and develop a thick skin, which I've had to do also.

I also pay attention to who I'm following—and unfollow energy vampires corrupting the way I think. I find the people who I most enjoy following on social media genuinely and authentically share the good in their lives, along with challenges or tough times. They are real people; they don't live behind the façade that everything is puppy dogs, sunshine, rainbows, and roller coasters.

I always warn people to not compare their insides to someone else's outside. Social media sometimes makes that difficult, however. Because comparison is the thief of joy, you must be discerning about when and how much social media you consume. Otherwise, you'll be constantly comparing yourself to everyone else's "life in social media." As we all know . . . that ain't REAL!

Another thing I don't take lightly is social media's addictive properties. We all know how tempting it is to check and interact on social networking sites throughout the day. Social media creators work extremely hard to make their apps so irresistible that you can't help checking them every hour—or every few minutes. Social networks use "clickbait" methods to draw you in, like seeing a red "7" on the Facebook notifications bar, signaling that seven people responded to your latest post. You have to know what they said about your latest vacation, right?

Because of social media's addictive nature, you could be staring at your phone instead of connecting with the person across from you because of FOMO—fear of missing out—on whatever is happening on your phone. Many people don't recognize this phenomenon in their own lives.

Others are mindlessly scrolling when they could be reading a good book, taking a nice walk—or working out in the gym! On top of that, I've seen too many families and too many couples sitting in a restaurant, looking at their phones while they wait for their meals to arrive. It breaks my heart to see this, which is why we have a rule in our family when we go to a restaurant: no phones on the table.

I realize that we can't unring the bell of social media. I'm guilty of being sucked in like everyone else. The habit may be impossible to kick, but you can set limits, like visiting social media sites once per day or keeping track of how much time you're spending with social media.

If you want to weaken your addiction, try this: stay away from social media from Friday afternoon to Monday morning. There have been times when I felt social media was robbing too much of my precious time and energy or draining my productivity, so

I took long weekend breaks and didn't post or read any social media content. I noticed that the world still spun on its axis after I disconnected from social media for a short time, and that will be the same for you.

But here's the hope I have, even for an activity that has so many pitfalls. For all its faults, I really believe social media can be a positive force in the world we live in. The ability to reach dozens, hundreds, thousands, and even millions is an incredible opportunity and a responsibility that I don't take lightly.

I want you to think of social media as "service media." Serve others online by providing authentic positivity. You can use your screen name for good by posting motivational quotes that stoke someone's spirit, by sharing pictures that inspire someone's creativity, and by writing heartfelt posts that make someone laugh and cry all at the same time.

Ask yourself, "Is this post going to create value for someone and potentially impact them positively?" If the answer is yes, then post away. Also make it a point *not* to engage in a confrontation, get into an argument, or say something negative in any of your posts.

You *can* use social media as a tool to serve others. When you do, you'll feel better, do better, and be better. That is how and why social media, when used properly, can be a great tool in your life. Service media goes a long way in getting minds right—your mind, and the minds of the people who follow you.

TAKE STEPS TO BECOME UBER-FOCUSED

So, Todd, with social media and everything coming at you, how do you stay focused and get everything done?

Listen, I get it. There are days when I get distracted and I'm not as focused as I need to be. What I aim to be now is uber-focused. This goal impacts how I spend my time, who I spend my time with, and the system I use for peak productivity.

I start with a fundamental understanding of what I *need* to focus on and not what I *want* to waste my focus on. Nothing is more helpful in this distinction than journaling. My focus "needs" are based on my priorities as well as my goals and the vision that I've mapped out for my life in my journal as well as my WLAG entries compiled each Sunday afternoon or evening.

I mentioned WLAGs before, which stands for Wins, Losses, Aha moments, and Goals. Let me share a sample from my Mother's Day entry in 2019:

My big three things for the week: #MyBig3

1. I need to make a big step forward on podcasting this week and recording an opening trailer.
2. We are building a house in Mexico on Saturday, and I'm super pumped for that.
3. I need to get another chapter done for my new book this week.

Here are my WLAGs:

Wins:

- Mom's Day today! Great day with brunch and church this AM. Excellent service as Pastor Miles McPherson interviewed four moms all with moving stories/lessons.
- Awesome P10 meeting on Monday & Tuesday in Baltimore. [P10 refers to my Power of 10 Mastermind group.] I really enjoyed spending time with all of them and thought we were very productive. Loved our time at Andrew Simpson's place and was very impressed.
- My day at Under Armour this week in Baltimore was just awesome. I had a blast being part of all that and bringing the P10 group there.

- FQ10 did great while I was away.
- I recorded a solid podcast with Pastor Jack Hawkins [with Canyon Springs Church in Scripps Ranch] on getting your mind right.
- I ordered microphones and equipment for doing my own podcast.

Losses:

- My team is losing the FQ10 Team Myzone Competition. We have to get everyone on the team to step up. We have a few people who have zero participation, and we can't win if they don't participate. We all need to step it up right NOW!
- Mike Chandler losing his Bellator MMA title in a controversial call. Now it's time to go back to work. Sometimes we do our best work when our backs are against the wall.

Aha Moments:

- I just can't be everything to everyone.
- I love competition. It's good for my soul. I'm enjoying this FQ10 Myzone Competition. But I don't like losing.
- I've got a ton of "big" things happening right now at the same time. Not only do I need to be on point, but I need the team to be dialed in also. We have a lot on our plate: podcasting, a book project, and several live event promos/marketing efforts to execute. Take one thing at a time. I have to majorly compartmentalize.

Goals:

- Fill out author survey for Baker Publishing.
- Attend Bo Eason event at end of week.

- Get ready to go to Mexico on Saturday to build a house for the poor. I'm looking forward to that.
- Garage workout on Tuesday with Joel Mountain at 12 noon. Go live during part of that.
- Order summer hoodies and giveaways for podcast launch.

I had a lot more bulleted items as well as a list of the important marketing initiatives, but you get the drift. Journaling what's important to me keeps me on task and serves as a reminder of what I want to accomplish in my lifetime, which is another way of saying, *What kind of legacy do I want to leave behind?*

Years ago, it was nothing for me to train thirty or forty hours a week. Nowadays, I train about ten hours a week because I have a lot more responsibilities than I did twenty years ago, ten years ago, or even five years ago. Leading my Fitness Quest 10 team and preparing and delivering keynote talks at various speaking gigs are important, but I'm mindful that my biggest responsibility is being a great husband and dad. This involves spending quality time with my wife of twenty years, Melanie, and making sure I schedule a special "date night" once a month. As for my kids, I'm the father of two teenagers and a preteen who will become young adults sooner than I expect, so I need to be there for them during the crucial adolescent years.

With all these responsibilities on my plate, I know that it takes a lot of focus to stay on task and see things through—while minimizing distractions at the same time. Here are some steps toward my uber-focused mindset that you can apply in your life as well:

1. Set up your environment for success. Most likely, you work in an enclosed office, cubicle, home office, or coffee shop. Wherever your workspace is, you should give some thought to creating an environment that will allow you to be more productive, stay focused, and feel less stressed at the end of the day.

I think the most important part of an office is your desk. Do you have enough room for your files, notes, and paperwork? Do you have drawers for your file folders? The goal is to *feel* like you're organized.

A few years ago, I knew that the one and only office at Fitness Quest 10 wasn't conducive to mapping out plans, composing blogs, or writing a book. Too cramped, too busy, and too many distractions. Melanie and I discussed options, and the best solution was turning one of our bedrooms into a home office for me.

I customized my home office exactly as I wanted it, including built-in cabinets, customized "can" lighting to brighten up my creative space, and a stand-up desk with a glass top so I could "white-board" on top of it. Man, I love my home office, and I do all my best work in there. And because I do my morning meditation and prayer time there, it really has become a sacred space for me.

2. Declutter your office. I've never forgotten what my mentor and author Wayne Cotton said one time: "You can't think big in a cluttered office."

He's right. I'm notorious for leaving a trail of "Durkin piles" wherever I go—a trait I inherited from my mother. There were times when I had stacks of papers, newspapers, and magazines piling up and cluttering my office to a point where I felt overwhelmed and couldn't think at all, let alone consider big thoughts. I feel so much more organized after I go through all those stacks and declutter, and you will too.

Decluttering pertains to your digital desktop as well. Get those single items organized into folders. Unsubscribe from newsletters and emails that no longer provide value, and get rid of phone apps that are cluttering your screen.

3. Pay attention to your environment. Green plants replenish oxygen in the air, so bring in a few plants for your home office, bedroom, and living spaces. Also, get a diffuser to experience aromatherapy in your office. Essential oils like lavender, rose, and sandalwood work at reducing stress and calming your senses.

Likewise, vanilla, peppermint, citrus, and cinnamon can heighten your senses, sharpen your mind, and increase energy.

4. Turn off "push" notifications, or better yet, turn off your phone. The number of emails and notifications we receive each day is staggering. According to a *Wall Street Journal* report, we're hit with sixty-three notifications and ninety emails daily, and we send forty emails each day. Those emails burn a lot of time, and steps must be taken—even radical ones.

When I'm in my peak productivity cycle, doing work that matters, my phone is turned completely off. I can't trust myself to ignore my emails as they come in. As for "push" notifications, it's amazing what social media apps as well as news and sports websites will do to get your eyeballs locked on them—which is how they make money, of course. You can turn off your notifications and still receive phone calls and text messages, but if you really want to be productive, turn that darned phone off.

Cal Newport, author of the book *Digital Minimalism,* says that turning your phone off for a few hours periodically throughout the day is a crucial step to allowing the brain some much-needed solitude time. Not getting this time can be characterized as "Solitude Deprivation Syndrome," which increases anxiety, impedes your creative juices, and doesn't allow you to flourish as designed. So think about turning your phone off for a couple of hours every day to get more solitude!

5. Put on noise-canceling headphones, for music or silence. Be choosy about the type of music you play through those headphones, though. While studies show that upbeat classical music helps creativity, I often go with "easy listening" tunes on Pandora or an "inspirational" playlist from my Apple music to get my mojo going.

I must confess, though, that I feel more creative when I have my headphones on with nothing playing. I love wearing my noise-canceling headphones and tuning the world out. This puts me in a "focus bubble" where I am inside myself instead of outside myself. I like my focus bubble, and I think you will too.

REVERSE ENGINEER YOUR SUCCESS

If you're ready to change things up and create the best year of your life, then I recommend that you reverse engineer your success, an idea I introduced in Key #3 but want to expand upon here.

What I mean by "reverse engineer" is that you should start with the big picture and move toward the daily steps: plan your year, plan your quarter, plan your month, plan your week, and then plan your day. Once that's done, you can win the day, win the week, win the month, win the quarter, and ultimately win the year. That's what reverse engineering your success is all about. Here are some tips to help make that happen:

• **Win the year by making out an Annual Roadmap & Strategic Plan.** I spend fifteen to twenty hours every December and early January framing up how I want to spend my time in the next year. I go through a hundred different questions about business and life and go deep on my vision and purpose in life. I then print out my Roadmap and have it spiral-bound. I review my Annual Roadmap & Strategic Plan periodically throughout the year because it serves as my compass for any big decisions.

• **Win the quarter with a 90-Day Wonder.** I learned this technique from Wayne Cotton twenty years ago. Every ninety days, I take an hour or two to ask myself three questions:

- What have I accomplished in the last ninety days?
- What are my current challenges, obstacles, and issues?
- What am I going to accomplish in the next ninety days?

I spend about twenty to thirty minutes on each section, sometimes longer. This allows me to review the last quarter, analyze where I am today, and then forecast the next quarter. I put an asterisk next to the areas or goals that are most important.

I really like working in ninety-day increments. It's a time increment that's long enough to be in a forecasting mode but short enough to see results.

• **Win the week with your WLAGs.** I've already described what my WLAGs are all about. Each Sunday, without fail, I share my wins and losses with my Fitness Quest 10 team and my Mastermind group, and I ask my leadership team to share theirs with me. This routine aids our communication. They know what I'm working on, and I have a good idea of what they're working on.

• **Win the day with the Big 5.** What are the five things that have to happen before I put my head on the pillow tonight to make sure I had a winning day? That's my mindset. When I go to bed with these five things done, I'm falling asleep with a smile on my face. Sure, there may have been a loss or two, but the sting wears off quickly.

LOOK FOR BLOCKS OF TIME

Here are some practical tactics that will help you take down your Big 5 for the day, whatever they may be:

1. **Start the day with the idea of "eat that frog."** What this means is that I try to do the most difficult or distasteful things early in the day, before my energy wanes and I put it off, saying, "I'll do it tomorrow."

2. **Don't try to do two ninety-minute blocks back-to-back.** To make wins happen with maximum focus, I've found that I like to work in ninety-minute blocks. If I can get two good ninety-minute blocks a day, that's three hours of high productivity on things that move my soul. If I happen to get in four blocks a day, that's huge because now I'm talking six hours of really focused attention to the tasks I set before me.

You need a minimum of twenty minutes between blocks. I'll go for a short walk, stretch, meditate, or do some breath work.

CHECK OUT MY "10 FORMS OF WEALTH" WHEEL AND THE "3-IN-30"

If you want to go deeper, I've come up with something I call the "10 Forms of Wealth Wheel":

10 Forms of Wealth

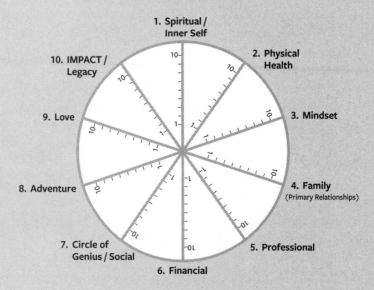

Notice the ten components for areas like your physical health, your spiritual self, your relationships, your career goals—ten different areas of life. What you do next is grade yourself on a 1–10 scale (10 being the best you could be) in each of the ten categories. This allows you to see areas of your life where you are strong and areas where you could use some improvement.

Next, you complete your 3-in-30. Write down three goals in each of the ten categories for the next thirty days (a one-month time frame). While that is a total of up to thirty goals (I sometimes suggest starting with a

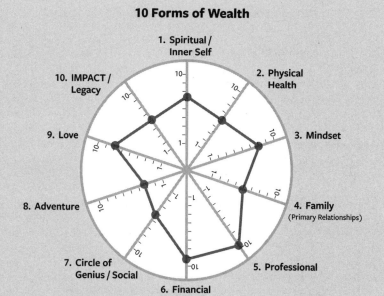

10 Forms of Wealth

1. Spiritual / Inner Self
2. Physical Health
3. Mindset
4. Family (Primary Relationships)
5. Professional
6. Financial
7. Circle of Genius / Social
8. Adventure
9. Love
10. IMPACT / Legacy

When you are ranking each area of your LIFE, keep in mind:

- 10 is where YOU want to be
- 10 is where you PICTURE yourself in a very near future
- 10 is your VISION of yourself
- 10 is your EXPECTATION for yourself
- 10 is what YOU feel you have in your tank

Rate yourself where you are TODAY, right NOW.
Pay attention to where there is disharmony or imbalance in the wheel.
Evaluate yourself each month. This exercise is a guaranteed GAME CHANGER.

"1-in-30"), it's not as daunting as it seems. You can up to five goals in one area. The aim is to get three strong goals per category. If you can put up to three goals in each of the ten areas for the next thirty days, watch what happens.

When you write down a goal on paper and declare it as a goal, you're more likely to accomplish what you set out to do and in all areas of your life. It's like the old saying: *Show me your calendar, and I'll show you your priorities.*

Here's an example of how 3-in-30 worked for me during the summer of 2019:

TD's 3-in-30

July 2019

Spiritual/Inner Life

1. Spend 15 minutes every AM in faith routine.
2. Church every Sunday (or listen via streaming if traveling).
3. Pray with Melanie & kids every night.

Physical Health

1. Minimum 30 minutes of workouts 5x per week. Burn 500 calories minimum per workout on the Myzone.
2. Clean nutrition; no sugar or processed foods 90 percent of the time; supplement routine dialed in.
3. Recovery amps up; at least 7 hours of sleep on at least 5 nights a week; 8+ hours 2 nights per week. Two massages this month.

Mindset

1. Listen to a podcast for at least 30 minutes, 5x per week while doing cardio.
2. Do NOT watch the news at all this month.
3. Zero naysayers or energy vampires in my circle.

Family

1. Attend McKenna's soccer tournament & Luke's lacrosse tournament.
2. Schedule a three-day escape with family.
3. No phones at breakfast table or dinner table.

Professional

1. Record 10 podcast episodes and get ready to release the "Todd Durkin IMPACT Show" podcast.
2. Crush it at IDEA World, Perform Better Long Beach, PB Providence, and Canfitpro.
3. Ten new members in the Mastermind.
4. Turn in book manuscript. ☺

Financial

1. Keep LEADING at Fitness Quest 10—feed culture, build leaders, shower praise continuously.
2. Deliver great value to all I coach and serve (clients, Mastermind group, social media).
3. Work on IMPACT Transformation Contest for 2020. Consumer-based coaching program/contest based on physical and life transformation.

Circle of Genius/Social

1. Date night with Melanie at least one time this month.
2. Mastermind time at IDEA World & coaching them this month!
3. Time with Pastor David Jeremiah this month.

Adventure

1. Two beach workouts.
2. Spa day with Melanie.
3. Hot Yoga class.

Love

1. Daddy/daughter date with McKenna.
2. Do an extra date with Melanie this month (no kids!).
3. Football training every week with Luke & Brady this month. I love this!

Impact/Legacy

1. Make *Getting Your Mind Right* as great as possible.
2. Be completely present with my NFL athletes this month as training camp starts in a few weeks; enjoy my time with them.
3. Inspire Mentorship attendees to GO DEEP, overcome fear, and be courageous to share their amazing gifts with the world. I derive much satisfaction in seeing my students create massive IMPACT in their respective communities.
4. Motivate & inspire the trainers/fit pros I work with this month. Help them create WOW & IMPACT in their life. Be bold. Speak with passion. Ignite them with energy. Radiate light and positivity.

There you go.

People often ask me, "What happens if you don't achieve your goals?"

The answer is, "Nothing." I don't feel guilty about it. I don't whine about it. I don't even feel bad about it. I just know that when you write your goals down and share them with your spouse, your family, or even teammates, you're much more likely to achieve happiness and harmony in your life.

The 10 Forms of Wealth and the 3-in-30s are something I do every month. It takes only fifteen to twenty minutes to complete but goes a long way in allowing me to focus my time on what's most important in my life.

The consuming thought in my mind is to follow my 1 percent rule: striving to get 1 percent better or more productive each day. Over a day, over a week, over a month, and over a quarter, I'm going to see real progress. You will too!

3. Instead of focusing on getting everything done, focus on just a few things with laser-like intensity. Then watch what happens to your productivity. This is how you "dominate the day" and feel great about everything you accomplish.

WHAT ARE THE FIVE THINGS THAT MOST MOVE YOUR SOUL?

Now that you're ready to focus, *what* should you be focusing on? How do you know what to invest your precious time and energy doing?

You have to be a master of your time, which will help you maximize your productivity, success, significance, and even happiness. And to master your time, you need to calibrate how you focus. Sounds simple, but so few can do it.

What I did was ask myself a key question: "What are the five things that most move my soul?"

I could list ten or more things, but I thought it was important to whittle the list down to five:

1. Writing
2. Speaking
3. Leading others
4. Training and coaching people
5. Having family time

Identify the five things that most move your soul, the things that you wish took up the majority of your time. Your list will depend on your occupation as well as your family situation. The point is, I want to help you figure out how to spend more of your time doing what you *love* to do, more of what moves your soul, and more of what is in line with your divine purpose.

If you can spend 80 percent of your time doing things that move your soul, then you're going to be more energized and more focused on the things you love to do. Organizing your time that

HOW DO YOU WIN THE DAY?

- Work in ninety-minute blocks. Make sure you turn off your phone and your email notifications during this time. This is completely distraction-free, focused work time.
- Don't forget that completing two blocks a day is good, and four blocks is great.
- Give yourself at least a twenty-minute break between blocks. Stand up, stretch, go for a walk around the block, check your email or social media, or connect with the people you work with.

Just don't forget to turn off those digital distractions before you go on to your next block.

way will allow you to be more creative, get more things done, and impact those around you.

DO YOU KNOW YOUR CYCLES?

This would be a good time to pay attention to your peak productivity cycles. I've found that if I don't heed mine, I'm not nearly as productive as I want to be.

We all have an internal twenty-four-hour clock running in the background as we sleep, wake up, go about our day, and prepare ourselves to fall asleep, which is known as our circadian rhythm. During each twenty-four-hour day, we cycle through times where we feel energized as well as times when we lack pep and are not at the top of our game. There are even times when we feel drowsy and could use a nap.

I know that I'm highly productive between seven in the morning (right after my workout) and noon. Another good spurt is from

4:00 to 6:00 PM. I also might get in a good cycle between 8:00 and 9:30 PM.

But early afternoon? On some days, you might as well stick a fork in me. And don't ask me to be creative after ten o'clock at night. I'm half-asleep, down for the count.

I have to create in the morning because that's when my energy is the highest and my mind is as right as it will ever be. After I've done my early morning routine, I'm juiced and ready to step into what I call my "genius zone"—my time of greatest creativity.

But you can't expect a "genius zone" to just happen—you have to make it happen with great planning.

CREATE YOUR IDEAL DAY AND WEEK

I've found that most people don't create their ideal day, week, or schedule. Instead, they react to what everyone else has going on—especially in social media—and before they know it, they're not focusing on their own lives. When that happens, energy wanes because so much cognitive effort is needed to deal with the horde of emails, notifications, and texts. I've seen it happen time and time again—it even happens to me.

I've taken some steps to rectify this. On Mondays, Wednesdays, and Fridays I train clients from 7:00 to 11:00 AM, working with people like pastor David Jeremiah, Drew Brees, and Tony Gwynn Jr.—and I don't have my smartphone near me. I'm creative and "on" during these times, so my clients get the best Todd possible.

I use Tuesday and Thursday mornings primarily as "writing and coaching" days from my home office. When I'm writing, I'll turn off my phone so I can block out everything and turn my attention to blogs, book chapters, or keynote addresses.

When I'm focused on coaching, I'm creating content on business, leadership, marketing, or personal growth for my Mastermind members. Or I'm leading a coaching call. Or creating my next retreat or live Mentorship event.

Mornings are the time when I'm clearheaded and able to crank it out. In the early afternoon, when I'm at a lower ebb, I'll do things that are mentally less taxing, like answering emails or catching up on my reading.

You may be entirely different. You may feel that you have to answer your emails *before* you can go to the genius zone and do the more creative aspects of your job. Maybe that's what gets your mind right, knowing that you're caught up on your phone calls, texts, and emails. You have to know what works best for you and create a schedule that reflects those rhythms. And then you have to work like mad to stick to your schedule.

What you're doing is creating structure, which involves three practices:

- discipline
- uber-focus
- resistance to distraction

These are your best practices. You can't just sit in a chair and expect the mind to be firing incredible thoughts without being aware of your peak productivity cycles and taking steps to protect them.

I'm reminded of Under Armour's first major ad campaign, which was called "Protect This House," referring to the training, sweat equity, and camaraderie that goes into being your best when it counts. Protect your house when it comes to safeguarding your most creative times of the day.

WTF

I'll finish with a fun story about a close friend and colleague, Trina Gray, who is the longest-standing member in my Todd Durkin Mastermind group and someone I've mentored for more than a dozen years. She owns a successful medically based health club, Bay Athletic Club, in her hometown of Alpena, Michigan, as well as Bay Urban Fitness, a personal fitness studio. She is the mom of two talented teens; is an amazing entrepreneur, coach, and community leader; and still has time to be involved in her church.

At one of my annual 3.5 Day Mentorship events, I asked Trina to speak on peak productivity and time management. Her topic was deepening productivity and focus, and as she got rolling, she stopped and looked at the hundred or so in the audience.

"Folks, we have a problem," she began. "It's called WTF."

Where is she going with this? I certainly knew what WTF was shorthand for in the texting world.

"Yes, I said WTF," she continued. "What the Focus is going on around here? Why is everyone chasing the shiny object in life? Why can't we focus on what needs to be done, when it's needed to be done, so we can stop complaining about what's *not* being done?"

My gasp turned into the biggest laugh. She was dead right. We often find ourselves chasing shiny objects that promise to accelerate our success, explode our revenues faster than ever, and even get us twelve-pack abs and a ripped body in a matter of weeks.

Come on, people. That takes our eyes off the ball. It's like what PGA-tour golfers will tell you about how they focus: *Think execution, not result.*

You'll never maximize your time or energy until you focus better than you ever have before. When you're focused, you're dialed in to how and what you're doing to accomplish your wins and aha moments, not lost in the future, thinking about what the results will be or the rewards you'll enjoy when things happen your way.

So there you have it—the Annual Roadmap & Strategic Plan, the 90-Day Wonder, the 10 Forms of Wealth, 3-in-30, WLAGs, and Big 5 for the day. These exercises will help you become a master of your time, energy, and focus and protect your peak productivity cycles.

So set your schedule, avoid distractions, and one more thing . . . WTF!

THIRD QUARTER

PERFORMING OPTIMALLY

In this third quarter, I will discuss training, nutrition, and recovery. While these all affect our physical energy, they also play an enormous role in our mental and chemical makeup and ultimately dictate if our mind is right.

They all take tremendous daily discipline. But if you include the techniques, tips, tactics, and hacks from this section, I promise you that your energy will thrive, your performance will prosper, and your life will soar.

Time to train smart, eat right, and recover like a champion!

KEY #6

Train to Win

I hated every minute of training, but I said, "Don't quit.
Suffer now and live the rest of your life as a champion."
—Muhammad Ali, heavyweight boxing champion

Do you not know that your bodies are temples of the
Holy Spirit? . . . Therefore honor God with your bodies.
—1 Corinthians 6:19–20

I *love* grey hoodies!

There's something about a grey hoodie that symbolizes what tough training is all about. I guess it goes back to the 1976 premiere of *Rocky.* I fell in love with this tough, underdog fighter from the streets of Philly. He had the spirit of a warrior, the work ethic of a mule, the mind of a champion . . . and I loved how Rocky wore a grey hoodie when running under damp early-morning skies.

That grey hoodie became imprinted in my DNA. The grey fabric reminds me of where I come from and the work ethic it takes to be a champion in all facets of life. Even today I wear my grey hoodie in many of my workouts.

Is my grey hoodie mandatory? No. Well, sometimes. It's optional.

When I really need to remind myself to amp up the training, dial up the intensity, and increase the focus, the grey hood gets flipped up. That's when I know it's time to get to work.

All the best athletes and champions I have worked with can flip that switch. I mean, not all of them wear hoodies, but they all have some way to signal that it's GO time. They are driven. They are single-minded. They will do what I ask them to achieve what they want. And they use training as a way to prepare themselves for the success they desire.

I've had the incredible opportunity to train hundreds of the most elite pro athletes in the world. I've also had the awesome opportunity to coach some of the most successful men and women on the planet, who are doing amazing things around the globe. This includes entrepreneurs, philanthropists, doctors, and even famous pastors.

I've noticed something: they all share the same mindset on training, conditioning, health, and fitness to reach their maximum potential. They train to win.

Asking me to name my favorite client would be like asking me to pick my favorite kid. It's impossible. But there is someone who is pretty special to me—"Dr. J." I'm not talking about the basketball player Julius Erving, who was known as "Dr. J" during his ABA and NBA career in the 1970s and '80s. Instead, I'm talking about Dr. David Jeremiah, the senior pastor of Shadow Mountain Community Church in El Cajon. He's also the voice of Turning Point, a broadcast ministry that airs his sermons and teachings on more than 2,000 radio and TV stations around the world and to millions online.

Dr. J has been coming to my gym three mornings a week at 7:00, when he's in town, for the last five years. I see my role clearly: keep his seventy-nine-year-old body strong and in great shape so that his mind stays sharp as a tack.

If you've ever read any of Dr. Jeremiah's books, including his most recent projects, *Everything You Need: 8 Essential Steps to a Life of Confidence in the Promises of God* and *The Book of Signs: 31 Undeniable Prophecies of the Apocalypse*, then you've been blessed by his incredible knowledge of the Bible and the insightful teaching on every page. If I can help extend his productive years, then I feel like I've fulfilled one of God's callings on *my* life. Heck, the fact that he dedicated his latest book, *Everything You Need*, to me was a great honor!

Dr. Jeremiah is one of the most passionate, successful, and impactful men I know, and he trains with as much intensity and focus as any of my pro athletes. He likes to arrive early, around 6:45 each morning, so that he can warm up on the treadmill before we get at it during our hour-long session. This is my opportunity to chat with him while he strides on the treadmill and gets his heart pumping. More often than not, I'll hear an interesting insight about the latest sermon he's preparing, or he'll share a profound nugget of wisdom.

HITTING THE SPEED-UP BUTTON

One morning, Dr. J was saying something really fascinating, but I couldn't hear him very well because of the noise inside the gym. I leaned in closer to pick up the next morsel, but unbeknownst to me, my right elbow accidentally leaned on the red "speed up" arrow on the treadmill. Suddenly, the treadmill shot up in speed from 3.5 mph to 8 mph.

When the treadmill motor kicked into a higher gear, the walking belt accelerated so fast that Dr. J broke into a sprint while he grabbed the handrails and hung on for dear life. A look of pure terror crossed his face as his legs churned like an Olympic sprinter. We both knew that if he slipped, the out-of-control treadmill belt would launch him into space and cause a serious injury.

All this happened in an instant, of course. I thank God that I had the presence of mind to quickly pull the emergency switch to cut the power. As the treadmill belt slowed to a crawl, Dr. J caught his breath and laughed. "I haven't run that fast in years," he joked.

Me? I wasn't chuckling because I had almost seriously injured one of the most famous pastors in America.

Two days later, I found Dr. J warming up on the treadmill before our workout. After teasing me not to inadvertently press the speed-up button, he shared this insight: "You know, Todd, sometimes in life, you need someone to hit your speed-up button. We all get caught up in ruts and doing the same routine over and over, but sometimes it takes an outside force to speed things up and show you a new perspective on life. Thanks for what you did on Monday."

Leave it to Dr. J to find a silver lining over the treadmill mishap, but the pastor raised a good point: Who needs a speed-up button when it comes to the amount of exercise we're doing each week? The reason I ask is because many say they don't have time to exercise. I understand why: careers are in full bloom; there are kids to raise, extracurricular activities to plan for, and vacations to plot; plus there's always someone asking us to volunteer for a community event or worthy cause.

Since something has to give in our schedules, the first thing that's usually tossed overboard is the time we set aside to exercise. Many play the fool and pretend they don't really need to work out, while others figure there's "always tomorrow" and that they'll get around to exercising sometime in the future. A hardy few figure out a way to include much-needed exercise time in their busy lives.

I don't want to wrestle you to the ground and make you promise to exercise regularly. What I hope to do is change your mindset about the importance as well as benefits of consistent exercise. If you choose to go through the rest of your days on earth without being intentional about how much and how often you exercise, you're likely choosing a shortened life span and lower quality of living.

That's why I implore you to get your mind in the right place *right now*. Do something about your fitness level while you still can. Why wait any longer? Even if your health has been going in the wrong direction for years, it's never too late to turn things around. I've seen people transform their lives at Fitness Quest 10 in incredible ways—young people, old people, and everyone in between—but each person shared a common mindset: *I've decided to do something about my health and my fitness level. Being out of shape is not good for me or my family. I've gotta get my mind right now.*

Perhaps deep down you know that you're not as fit as you could be. Sure, you've added weight over the years and aren't as spry as you once were, but you chalked that up to the passage of time, something as inevitable as the next robocall.

Well, I have news for you: you can turn back the hands of your body clock. Sure, aging is inevitable and time waits for no one. But that doesn't mean you have to shuffle off into the sunset, grasping a cane and looking for the nearest park bench to settle into. You can still regain lost years if you start exercising today.

Let's get our minds right by remembering that we have much to live for: our immediate family, our grandchildren, our friends, our careers, our hobbies, our pastimes, our love for travel, and our opportunities to minister to others. One of the most satisfying things we've done as a family in the last year was to travel to Tijuana to help out with the construction of a Build a Miracle home. Not only did my children and I feel like we made a real difference in a family's life, but we got our minds right about the incredible blessings we have—like our own house.

Seize the opportunity to make a difference in your life as well. *Now* is the time to climb aboard the fitness bandwagon. Whether you're just starting out, you're jumping back on the bandwagon, or you're a serious fitness enthusiast, I'm confident that the ten steps below will help you improve your strength, energy, conditioning, and yes, even your mindset.

Let's get training!

1. BREAK A SWEAT MOST DAYS OF THE WEEK

The question I hear the most at Fitness Quest 10 is this: *Hey, Todd. How many times should I work out in a week?* I think it's because people want to know what's the minimum amount of exercise they can get away with.

My standard answer is short and succinct: "I recommend you sweat most days of the week and combine lifting weights, conditioning, and flexibility to help get your body and mind right."

The American Heart Association recommends 150 minutes a week, which is not that much time when you break it down. Actually, I view 150 minutes—thirty minutes a day, five days a week—as a baseline. The longer you work out, the healthier you're going to be.

At least half that time should be spent performing high-intensity exercise because a dose of intense training will give you a quartet of neurotransmitters that are released by the brain. I'm referring to a jolt of DOSE: dopamine, oxytocin, serotonin, and endorphins.

These "happy chemicals" get your mind right for the day ahead, if you work out in the early morning hours. If you prefer to exercise after your workday is over, they settle your mind for a good night's sleep. The most important point about this DOSE of chemicals is that they help you as much mentally as they do physically.

The most important thing to think about right now is which days you plan to exercise. I'm hoping that you'll commit to doing *some* form of exercise thirty minutes a day, five days a week, and work up from there. Include time for high-intensity interval training, which is short bursts of intense exercise, but make sure you alternate or vary your high-intensity interval training with more moderate aerobic activity.

Ready to move forward? Good, because there are three forms of exercise you want to incorporate into your weekly schedule:

A. Cardio/aerobic exercise. This form of exercise causes the body to utilize oxygen to create energy. Expressed another way, the body is said to be working aerobically when the cardiorespiratory system—the heart, the lungs, and the bloodstream—is replenishing energy as you exercise. Examples of aerobic exercise are

- walking
- jogging
- swimming
- rowing
- using treadmills, stair steppers, and elliptical machines
- riding spin bikes, stationary bikes, mountain bikes, or road bikes
- playing high-energy games of tennis, racquetball, basketball, volleyball, etc.

While steady-state "cardio" has taken a bad rap the last several years, I'm still a believer. Cardio has a positive effect on the heart and lungs, burns fat, and gives you that great post-workout feeling.

B. Anaerobic exercise. The new vogue terminology for this is "high-intensity interval training" (HIIT), which pairs strength-training exercises and challenges the body's lactate-threshold system. Lactic acid is the by-product of intense exercise and has been shown to spike hormones like testosterone, growth hormone, and IGF-1, which are all responsible for increasing strength, losing body fat, and changing body composition.

High-intensity interval training, or anaerobic exercise, causes the body to make energy without oxygen because the demand for energy is so intense. Examples of anaerobic exercise are

- strength training while lifting weights or using machines
- body-weight strength exercises like squats, lunges, push-ups, pull-ups, sit-ups, lunge-hops, squat jumps, and burpees

- sprint training—for example, complete one 400-meter run, two 200-meter runs, three 100-meter runs, and six 40-yard dashes—whew!

If you're looking to get stronger, lose weight, and change your body composition, high-intensity interval training needs to be part of your routine two to three times per week for a minimum of twenty minutes. Complete all that and check in with me in ninety days. I bet you'll love the way you look and feel.

C. Stretching/flexibility. Adding this component to your workout is a game changer. The ability to increase range of motion, break down scar tissue, and lengthen muscles is tremendous for the body and underutilized in many workout programs. Stretching and flexibility exercises give your body a chance to recover from your more strenuous workouts.

I would recommend stretching for at least ten minutes after your workouts and fifteen minutes before you go to bed. If that's all you do, your flexibility will improve, your body will recover faster, and you'll feel a lot better.

Getting a sweat going throughout the week involves a combination of all three approaches—cardio, anaerobic, and stretching. I want you to get that heart pumping, like taking a brisk walk or jog around the neighborhood, cycling on a stationary bike, or pumping your arms and legs on an elliptical machine a couple of days a week. Then take it up a notch—do high-intensity interval strength training every other day to get stronger and rev up your metabolism. And on the fifth day, you'll find yourself in a yoga class, where the stretching exercises increase your range of motion, prevent muscle strain, keep your circulation levels high, and allow you to gently recover from your other workouts.

The most important thing is that you do something physical nearly every day to get that daily DOSE. As ancient Greek philosopher Thales once said, "A sound body is a sound mind."

Twenty-five hundred years later, those words still ring true.

2. TRICK THE BRAIN—AND WAKE UP!

First thing in the morning can mean different things to different people. Even though 5:00 AM comes early for many folks, I have no trouble getting up at that time. Since I need approximately sixty minutes to complete my morning routine, I don't want to be rushed before I start my regular day.

I will admit, though, that there have been times when I've woken up and heard a voice in my head say, *I don't feel like exercising today* or *I've got too much to do to work out.*

When that happens, I'll play a little trick on myself by saying, *Okay, then I'll go on a fifteen-minute walk.* My companion is Jersey, our golden retriever, who needs his morning walk anyway.

What usually happens is that I walk much longer and return to the house thirty to forty minutes later wearing a sweaty grey hoodie and ready to get into my home gym for my main workout. It's incredible how often a fifteen-minute stroll turns into a half hour or so of good cardio.

Here's what I want you to do the next time you feel pressed for time: tell yourself that you're only going to do fifteen minutes of exercise and see what happens. I'm confident that once you break a sweat, you'll want to keep going longer than you originally planned to work out.

Another trick I play on myself is to check my numbers. What I mean is that if I can see how many calories I've burned in the last half hour or what heart rate zone I'm in, that's enough motivation to keep my head in the exercise game. To keep tabs on those numbers, I wear a Myzone heart rate monitor—a strap that wraps around my upper chest and provides real-time feedback on my heart rate, the number of calories I've burned, and how much effort I'm putting into my exercise program that day.

I absolutely love it when I find out that I just burned 400, 500, or even 600 calories during a morning workout in my home gym, meaning I can put that much fuel right back into my body.

143

(Translation: I can eat my oatmeal and eggs without feeling guilty.) Not only is a heart rate monitor a great motivational tool, but that strap around my chest provides accountability. Another trick I play is telling myself that I need to burn at least 400 calories in the early morning before I do anything else.

The Myzone monitor also tells me the percentage of the time I spend in a certain heart rate zone. I know if my activity is as intense as it needs to be. There are five different colored zones:

- the **gray zone** is when I'm in the 50–59 percent zone of my MHR (maximum heart rate)
- the **blue zone** is when I'm in the 60–69 percent zone of my MHR
- the **green zone** is when I'm in the 70–79 percent zone of my MHR
- the **yellow zone** is when I'm in the 80–89 percent zone of my MHR
- the **red zone** is when I'm in the 90–100 percent zone of my MHR

When I'm taking a solitude walk—which I also call a "gratitude walk"—with or without Jersey, I like to be in the blue or green zone, somewhere in the 65 to 75 percent range. When I'm pumping iron, I like to see periods in the green and yellow zone. And when I'm out doing sprints or an intense interval circuit, I want to be in the yellow and red zones.

It's a great tool for the whole community too. At Fitness Quest 10, everyone who's wearing a Myzone strap can be linked wirelessly to our main computer, and the results are tabulated and posted on TV monitors around the gym. If thirty people are strapped to a Myzone monitor, and most of them are in the green zone while eight colleagues are in the yellow and red maximum heart rate zone, those people in the blue zone should be inspired to pick it up and get huffing and puffing.

I also use the Myzone to track the athletes I train, even when they're not at Fitness Quest 10. If a certain NFL player is vacationing in Hawaii during the off-season but is starting to get back in shape for a team minicamp, or if he goes on a jog or lifts weights at a nearby gym and he's wearing a Myzone strap, I can see how many calories he's burning and what maximum heart rate zone he's in through an app on my phone. Amazing technology.

How about using this technology to motivate your workout? No matter what your age is, it can be motivating to quantify your training zones, maximum heart rate, and the effort you're putting into your workout.

Remember this: you have to break a sweat most days of the week. While I prefer to work out during the most magical time of the day, just be sure to get your sweat in sometime during your waking hours and you'll experience the exact same effects.

3. REMEMBER THAT MUSCLE IS MAGIC AND MOTION IS LOTION

Let me tell you about Bob Hill.

He's been training with me for twenty years for at least one day a week, and he sets aside at least two additional days a week for strength training.

Why? Because he still wants to look good. He still wants to feel good. And as a single man, he still wants to date.

Did I tell you that Bob is seventy-eight years old?

Bob understands that at his age—and this applies to everybody—strengthening his muscles is absolutely essential, because we all lose muscle mass as we grow older. Between the ages of forty and sixty, we lose an average of a half pound of muscle and gain about a pound of fat each year, if we do nothing on the fitness front. In addition, the loss of muscle and bone mass leads to the deterioration of our internal organs and our cardiovascular systems as we get older.

Why is muscle so important?

- Having strong, healthy muscles is necessary to perform everyday activities. That's why we call it functional fitness.
- Strength training increases lean body mass, which is made up of your bones, ligaments, tendons, internal organs, and muscles. When you have more lean body mass, your clothes fit better and you look better.

Two days of strength training a week is a good goal to set, although three is even better. Spending twenty to thirty minutes at a time is often all you need. If you don't belong to a gym at the moment, body-weight exercises such as planks, push-ups, squats, pull-ups, and lunges can give you a phenomenal workout anywhere. While I love the energy environment you'll find in a gym, fitness studio, or health club, you can push, pull, squat, hip-hinge, and plank at home. Bottom line is that you have to get it in.

Most of us have enough body weight to get in some great strength training. But if you would like to amp it up even more, here are some of my other favorite exercise tools:

- dumbbells
- barbells and weights
- kettlebells
- TRX suspension trainer
- super bands
- sport cords

These are the mainstays of many of my workouts as well as my "tools of the trade" when I train a teen, a parent, a professional athlete, Pastor Jeremiah, or Bob Hill.

Get out there and move your body. Build muscle and get strong. Not only will you get physically stronger, you will benefit from mental magic as well.

4. GO FOR CIRCUIT TRAINING

One of the methodologies I love to incorporate during my workouts is circuits. By this, I mean grouping two or three strength and conditioning exercises together and completing a circuit for a set number of rounds or for a specific period of time.

I use this methodology with most of my clients because it's time-efficient, effective, and keeps things metabolically challenging. Circuits allow for improvement in strength, power, and conditioning, and you can get through two to three of them in less than twenty minutes.

Here are three examples of basic circuits:

Circuit #1: Bodyweight Blast

1. Pushups (10)
2. Squats (20)
3. Jumping jacks (30)
   Complete three rounds.

Circuit #2: Energy Up!

1. Walking lunges (20)
2. Flexed arm hangs (for as long as possible)
3. Plank (one minute)
   Complete three rounds.

Circuit #3: MindRight Maniac

1. Kettlebell swings (10)
2. TRX rows (10)
3. Burpees (10)
   Complete as many rounds as possible in five minutes.

Note: I have these circuits, along with seven additional circuits with descriptions and videos, available at www.ToddDurkin.com /GetYourMindRight.

To further amp up your results, you can get out and do a twenty-minute walk, jog, or run in the morning, come back to the house or gym, and complete twenty minutes of strength-based circuits. Your goal is to get in strength training three times per week for twenty to thirty minutes each time. If you do this, I promise you that your body composition will change and your mind will be on fire.

5. FLEXIBILITY AND FASCIA WILL HELP YOU FEEL GOOD

Back in another life, I was a professional football player trying to make it to the NFL by playing in European football leagues. My dream ended in Aix-en-Provence, France, when two linebackers nailed me at full speed after I ran out of the pocket. I can still feel their helmets crunching bone and cartilage in my lower back. Ouch!

My back was heavily damaged. Doctors couldn't help me. Not when they determined that I had three herniated disks, spinal stenosis, and the degenerative spinal column of a seventy-five-year-old, even though I was just twenty-five years old.

I came home to the States two months later and needed painkillers every day to survive. I couldn't move. I needed help in a big way.

My sister Patti told me about this guy named Dub Leigh who was an expert in massage and bodywork. Figuring I had nothing to lose, I went for it. He dug his fingers and elbows into my hip rotators and places in my back that I didn't know existed. Man, that stuff hurt.

But you know what? Dub Leigh helped me turn a corner. My back got a lot better. I got a lot more flexible in my hips because of Dub's work. And I discovered fascia.

Fascia is a cobweb-like substance intertwined around every muscle, tendon, ligament, nerve, and bone in our bodies. This glue-like tissue connects us from our feet to our fingertips, left and right, front and back. We are one big fascial sheath, which is why I believe fascia holds on to the physical, mental, emotional, and spiritual pain and trauma of the body. A lot of that gunk is stored in our fascia, so if we don't get rid of it, it will fester and show itself eventually as disease.

If you have a hurting back like I had, or hips that are tight, or headaches, or plantar fasciitis in your feet, then you're a candidate for bodywork and deep-tissue massage to get rid of the gunk in your fascia and improve your flexibility and mobility. Foam rolling, a form of self-massage that I'm also a fan of, increases blood flow and gets rid of adhesions and other "knots" in your muscles.

There are differences between flexibility and mobility, both of which play an important role in overall health and feeling good. Flexibility comes from lengthening muscle, while mobility comes from increasing range of motion through joints in the hips, the shoulders, or the extremities.

The older we get, the more time we need to spend on our flexibility and mobility routines. My challenge to you is to perform a minimum of ten minutes of stretching or mobility work each day.

Note: I have my Top 7 stretches, with accompanying descriptions and videos, available at www.ToddDurkin.com/GetYour MindRight.

6. ADOPT A "NO EXCUSE" POLICY

For the three years leading up to my partial knee replacement surgery, I wasn't able to run, squat, or lunge. But that didn't mean I couldn't do push-ups, bench presses, lat pulldowns, TRX exercises, core work, or even a little "arm farm" with dumbbells. Even though I had knee issues, I didn't miss workouts.

I knew the mental positive side effects of exercise were mandatory in my personal routine. It wasn't a matter of *if* I was going to keep exercising. It was just a matter of *what* I would do to work around the pain.

Many people have pain in their bodies like I did. I understand how lingering aches and pains affect you mentally, if you let them. If you don't exercise, however, your aches and pains will send you further down a spiraling abyss of negativity or depression.

Get moving today, even if you're dealing with pain. If you have an ailment in your upper body, then train your lower body. If your lower body is injured, then be sure to train your upper body. Focus on things you can do versus what you *can't* do.

If you're seeing a physical therapist, physician, or chiropractor while rehabbing from an injury, keep training the entire body so you can address your whole being. After all, you are far more than a knee, a shoulder, or a back.

7. EXERCISE WITH THAT SPECIAL PERSON IN YOUR LIFE . . . AND JOIN A GYM

Training with a spouse, doing a yoga class together, or going for a walk together is a great way to exercise while "checking in" with your significant other. I love working out with Melanie, whether we are doing a weight-training workout or taking a stroll through the neighborhood with Jersey. Life's distractions fall by the way-side and we can talk about the kids' schedules, what's coming up, and future getaways. Just as a family who prays together stays together, I believe that every couple who sweats together stays together as well.

Speaking of relationship, that's one reason I believe in the power of joining a gym: community. Whether you join as a family, a part-nership, or solo, when you join the right studio, club, or gym, you're becoming part of a group of like-minded individuals who share a common desire for better health, happiness, and prosperity.

The friends and connections you make at the gym often go way beyond the class or session that you share together. There is often a bond and camaraderie that is formed only on teams and at gyms. That's the power of sweating together!

8. DIVERSIFY YOUR ROUTINE—AND DON'T FORGET ABOUT THE POWER OF NATURE

Diversifying your routine is an important aspect of training to win because people tend to get in a rut and stay there. Those who do Pilates just do Pilates. Those who lift always lift. And those who never miss a yoga class stick to yoga.

You gotta shake things up. Doing the same old workout is not only boring but can also prevent you from reaching your fitness goals. The key word to keep in mind is *cross-training*, which is a combination of activities such as weight lifting, aerobic exercise (walking, jogging, running, cycling, swimming), yoga, and Pilates. Alternating the activities you do each day will heighten your fitness level and protect you from injuries and pain. Once again, this is another reason to join a great studio, club, or gym that has an array of offerings to keep you physically and mentally challenged.

And don't forget the bounty of nature. I love to mix it up in the mountains, which is good for the body, mind, and soul. I do my biggest and best thinking when I'm in the mountains of Colorado or Utah, where the jagged peaks are dotted with snowbanks, even in the summer. I'm always inspired to think about how I can expand my business, grow my Mastermind group, and use social media to get the word out.

Most of us don't live in Colorado and Utah; we can't step outside our homes and see these beautiful and awe-inspiring mountains. But no matter where you live—near the ocean, near a lakeshore, near a nature reserve, or in a major metropolitan area—you can go for a walk, a hike, or a bike ride through a park or someplace scenic. If you don't have a go-to, find one!

9. WHEN THE WEATHER TURNS COLD AND NASTY, GO OUTSIDE

Shake things up when the weather turns rainy and cold. You may think I'm crazy, but some of my most memorable workouts have been going on a track workout or bleacher run when it was freezing rain or snowing outside.

When the weather gets ugly, I like to put on my oldest running shoes, slip on a grey hoodie and a beanie, and pop out the front door knowing I'll get soaking wet and cold. But man, do I feel good about myself when I return. I change my mindset from, *Oh, it's raining. I can't go outside* . . . to *There's nothing better than running in a rainstorm and feeling alive.*

The next time it rains or gets cold, don't stay inside. Go for a long walk, a fun run, or enjoy your favorite outside activity. Sometimes you gotta experience the elements to fully awaken your senses.

Try it—you might just like it.

10. GET GOOD COACHING—IT'S WORTH THE INVESTMENT

Throughout my career in the fitness world, I have not strived to be the best personal trainer. I've aimed to be the best coach.

Coaches inspire.

Coaches motivate.

Coaches get people better.

And that's what I want you to do—get better in everything you do!

When I speak to a group of personal trainers and coaches, I tell them that a good coach not only changes the way someone physically performs, they change the way that person mentally performs. Anyone can hold a clipboard and count reps, but a good coach changes lives, creates futures, refines goals, and leads the way. I've always believed in the power of a coach for the same reasons pro athletes come to me: we all need a coach to take us to the next level.

A great coach understands what motivates you and has a vision for your future, so a great coach makes you do what you don't want to do so that you can achieve what you always wanted to

WHAT ARE YOUR THREE MOST EUPHORIC WORKOUTS?

Can you think of three workouts—or sport activities—that were epic in your mind?

Here are my top three. I'll never forget the time I was downhill skiing in Deer Valley, Utah, flying down the mountain while recording a video on my iPhone for my Instagram followers. Then there was the time I led a beach workout with all my NFL guys, feeling the July heat as our feet sank in the sand. Last, there was the morning I went snowshoeing in Park City, Utah, in January, which afforded me the chance to experience the solitude and peacefulness of a blanket of virgin snow.

All of them are associated with nature, so get out and enjoy Mother Nature—she's good for the soul!

be. Former Dallas Cowboys football coach Tom Landry nailed it when he said, "A coach is someone who tells you what you don't want to hear, who has you see what you don't want to see, so you can be who you have always known you could be."

Just so you know, I'm not talking about hiring a personal trainer only to coach you to better fitness. I'm talking about hiring a trainer to help you work around those aches, ailments, and injuries I discussed earlier and get your mind right as well. Seek out a great coach near you and watch how your training appointments quickly impact all areas of your life.

Coaching goes beyond fitness too. Maybe you need a life coach, a business coach, a financial coach, or a spiritual coach. So let me ask you this: Where do you need the most help? Is it in your leadership within your career? Do you need to boost your self-confidence? Build more effective communication skills? Enhance your work performance?

I've always sought out good coaching for myself personally and professionally. I've attended plenty of "coaching seminars" over the years and have paid top dollar to hear premium speakers like Tony Robbins, Robin Sharma, Ali Brown, and Joe Polish share their insights about what it takes to be successful in today's world. I've had coaches work with me on my nutrition. I've had coaches in business. And I've had mentors and coaches help me with my spiritual walk and growing my faith.

One of the reasons I believe in coaching so much is because I believe in the "growth mindset" and have a continual thirst for learning. This is why I dig into self-help books and listen to podcasts from so-called thought leaders.

I'm a coach to other entrepreneurs, high performers, and fitness pros, and I want to be the best business and life coach I can be for those I mentor. For nearly fifteen years I've led my own Mastermind group and coached around two hundred fitness facility owners, leaders, and trainers with live retreats, monthly coaching calls, webinars, a Facebook private group, and a "members only" website filled with exclusive content. Additionally, I have multiple coaching programs that I take great pride in to help other "growth mindset" people seeking high performance.

You can go only as far as you can grow.

A CLOSING THOUGHT

Let me finish this chapter by telling a story about basketball coaching legend John Wooden, whose coaching philosophy was enshrined in his book *The Pyramid of Success*. On his deathbed, Coach Wooden was asked if there was anything he wanted changed in the book before he passed away.

"I wouldn't change any of the words," said the man who wrote, "Discipline yourself, and others won't need to."

But Coach Wooden did say he made a mistake when he made his famous "Pyramid of Success." The words along the bottom

COACH'S CORNER

I've seen the benefit of coaching from both sides. Not only have I witnessed incredible growth in my life, but I've seen hundreds of lives changed and thousands of lives impacted because of the power of coaching. I believe all great coaches have seven things in common:

1. Coaches care. I love this saying: "People don't care how much you know until they know how much you care."

2. Coaches listen. Great coaches listen twice as much as they speak. When they open their mouths, their speech is full of wisdom and experience.

3. Coaches hold you accountable. Not only do great coaches provide guidelines, show you the correct exercises, and give you a list of items to work on, but they hold you accountable for your actions.

4. Coaches motivate you. Great coaches know where to find the right buttons to push.

5. Coaches are growth-minded. Great coaches don't rest on their laurels. They continue to grow and learn.

6. Coaches have a champion's mindset. Winning begets winning, just as losing begets losing.

7. Coaches love helping people. Great coaches have a strong sense of purpose and mission—it's their calling. That's why they love helping people.

of the pyramid—the foundation of competitive greatness—were these nouns: industriousness, friendship, loyalty, cooperation, and enthusiasm.

One more noun should have been part of this cornerstone, he said.

That word was *love*.

"I could never have won all those championships if it wasn't for love. Me loving my players, and my players loving the cause they were playing for."

Wow.

You have a cause to play for—getting in the best shape of your life . . . now! There are no excuses. You can work around any limitations you may have. You can train and exercise as much for your mental framework as your physical results. When you don't feel like doing it, do it anyway. Your best workouts are the ones you don't feel like doing. The resulting sense of accomplishment, coupled with the endorphins and hormones released from the session, leave you in a state of near euphoria.

I want you to think about what you should commit to in your training routine. I promise you, the investment you make will be the best investment ever. I want you feeling like a million bucks. All you need to do is get started. Go ahead and set a scary goal of running a 5K, 10K, or a Spartan run. Whatever it takes to get out of a rut, I want you to commit to elevating your training game.

So put on a grey hoodie, get out the *Rocky IV* soundtrack, and start banging out some push-ups.

I'll see you in the gym—but be careful. I might lean on your "speed-up" button!

KEY #7

Eat Right to Get Your Mind Right

Let food be thy medicine and medicine be thy food.

—Hippocrates, ancient Greek doctor

When I was growing up, my mom served the same thing nearly every night: pasta and bread.

For eight hungry stomachs sitting around the dinner table, a heaping platter of boiled spaghetti or rigatoni and a steaming pot of tomato sauce always hit the spot. A basket filled with slices of baguette bread—which I slathered with butter—was passed around to fill us up between bites of delicious pasta. I loved our carbohydrate-rich meals, never aware that Mom was doing her best to stretch her food dollar. Meatless pasta and bread was one of the cheapest meals she could serve, especially when fast-growing kids were hungry for seconds and thirds.

Pasta remained a favorite of mine after I went to college and moved into my twenties. When Melanie and I started dating, I quickly learned that she could make great spaghetti with a meat

157

sauce that was out of this world. Pasta, red sauce, and a loaf of bread became a go-to meal for us after we married, although by this time I had added lots of veggies and great salads to my diet. I still loved buttered bread with dinner, however, and I got into a routine of not eating enough during my long workday. I'd come home ravenously hungry and end up eating too many carbs at night. And I convinced myself that I deserved dessert most nights of the week.

We'd been married for around five years when I noticed that I was tipping the scales at 225 pounds—a great weight if I was still playing football but a recipe for middle-age obesity if I wasn't careful. I had to get serious about my nutrition not only to change my bulky body, but to boost my energy and keep my mind alert.

Since that revelation fifteen years ago, I've gone through a whole nutrition paradigm shift. I've read books on the topic, enlisted meal prep companies to help me with quick lunches on the go, dropped the bread and extra carbs at dinner, and rarely eat dessert. I've dropped around twenty-five pounds after making these changes.

These days, my weight fluctuates between 197 and 205 pounds. All these years later, I realize now more than ever that if I'm not eating right, then I'm not going to feel good or be good. My mind won't be right, and I won't have my health, energy, and vitality. And without those things, I don't have anything.

We need to get our minds right about what we eat and drink. Good health is a lot more than not being sick most of the time or avoiding major diseases. Good health is waking up in the morning, ready to break a sweat and attack the day. Good health is having the energy and vibrance to put in an honest day's work and keep up with those kids you're raising. Good health is thriving, not merely surviving.

I've also learned about the importance of eating for brain health. I used to think during my carb-loading days that all the pasta and bread was fueling my body. The reality is that junky carbs are bad fuel. What I learned when I started making nutritional changes was that I needed a diet rich in whole grains, green leafy vegetables, avocados, and nuts. These are the types of foods strongly associated with better memory and a lower risk of developing Alzheimer's disease. Eating nutritious food is not only a smart thing to do, eating the right foods *today* sets me up for success *tomorrow* and decades to come. I want you to hear this message as well.

This chapter will only scratch the surface. You can find dozens of books at your local bookstore on the topic of good nutrition. I'm not going to tell you whether keto, Atkins, or paleo diets are good for you. What I've realized is that most people haven't even mastered the basics of good nutrition, so the better route to go is to acquire a fundamental knowledge of a proper diet. You'll feel better, look better, and your mind will be better. Your energy will skyrocket, your focus will be sharper, and you will be fueled for success.

In this chapter, I will share my Big 6 tips for eating right that will help you get your mind and body right. Don't skim these pages. The topic of nutrition is important, but I also believe that food and drink are to be enjoyed and celebrated.

So let's get started, and *bon appétit*.

BIG TIP #1: HYDRATE FOR SUCCESS

Believe me, I know when I haven't consumed enough water during the day.

That's when I wake up in the middle of the night with the most painful leg cramp ever. When a muscle spasms in one of my quads or hamstrings at one or two in the morning, I nearly hit the roof because the pain is so sharp and intense.

"Oh, my leg! My leg!"

I've woken up Melanie with one of my legs straight up in the air, searching for a body position that will lessen the cramp. If the cramp doesn't go away, then she'll help me get to the floor, where I'll writhe in pain until my cramp dissipates. Once that happens, I'll do some stretching and drink a big glass of water right away. Sometimes I'll add a dash of Himalayan sea salt or reach for an electrolyte drink.

When it comes to hydration, water is always my best option. Water is the perfect fluid replacement—an odorless, colorless, calorie-free, and sugar-free substance that regulates body temperature, transports nutrients and oxygen to the cells, protects organs and tissues, removes toxins in the body, and helps you maintain strength and endurance.

The problem is that people don't drink enough water, and the other liquids they do consume aren't nearly as healthy for them— I'm thinking of sodas, sugary juices, and mocha coffees topped with caramel and whipped cream. Replenishing the body with pure water is vitally important to our health because of the way the body uses fluids to eliminate waste products and cool the body.

So how much water should you drink during the day? Here's the simple answer: more than you're drinking now. I know every health book out there says drink "eight glasses a day," but that isn't realistic for most folks because they won't take the time to pour themselves three glasses of water a day, let alone eight. Many think they'll spend all day in the bathroom if they drink that much water. The fact of the matter is that your body is made up of 66 percent water, so you need more than you think.

A good rule of thumb for minimum hydration is one ounce of water for half your body weight. Since I usually weigh around 200 pounds, I should drink 100 ounces of water daily when I'm not exercising diligently and considerably more if I'm working out like a banshee. That's right around a dozen glasses of water.

Water, an incredible resource created by God, does many wonderful things for the body:

- **Minimizes joint pain.** Adequate water consumption lubricates the joints and can prevent gout attacks.

- **Helps with digestion.** Water helps break down food in the digestive tract so that the body can more readily absorb the nutrients. Water also softens stool, which prevents constipation.
- **Aids organ functions.** Water lessens the burden on the kidneys and liver by flushing out waste products. Nearly all the major systems in the body depend on water for their function.
- **Reduces headaches.** If you're fighting a tension headache, which feels like a tightening or pressure sensation in your head, that's a sign you're dehydrated.
- **Helps you make better cognitive decisions while clearing brain fog.** Science tells us that water plays a major role in brain function and that approximately 75 percent of the processes that take place in the brain occur in the presence of water. Brain fog is not a medical diagnosis but refers to symptoms like poor concentration, mental confusion, and decrease in intellectual productivity.
- **Improves your workouts and results.** Back in the day, football players were told to "suck it up" by going through an entire practice without taking a sip of water. Bear Bryant, the legendary coach for the Alabama Crimson Tide, banned water breaks as a test of toughness.

  Coach Bryant may have thought he was making his football players tough as nails, but all he was doing was running them into the ground. I've told my athletes that a body without enough water in the tank would be like trying to run a car without oil. You might be able to turn the engine on, but you won't get very far before you break down. The body needs constant hydration, and that hydration should come from drinking water, the best resource out there.
- **Builds muscles.** Water is absolutely necessary to build muscle because of the way it helps form the structures

161

of protein. In addition, muscles are controlled by nerve impulses, so the electrical stimulation of nerves and the contraction of muscles during a weight-lifting session, for instance, are dependent upon water and electrolytes. Protein synthesis is needed for muscle growth, but you'll never be able to build muscle if there isn't adequate water present to jump-start the synthesis of protein in the body.

- **Reduces stress levels.** Studies show that being dehydrated can increase your cortisol levels, a stress hormone, so drinking enough water will keep your stress levels down. The trouble is that many forget to drink water when they're under stress at work or at home. The next time you're feeling like the weight of the world is atop your shoulders, reach for a bottle of water.

When it comes to hydration, remember that these beverages don't do as much for you as plain old water: coffee, tea, alcoholic beverages, sports drinks, energy drinks, milk, flavored water, juice, and sodas.

Finally, how can you tell if you're properly hydrated?

First, if you're hydrated, you're not thirsty. When you're thirsty, the brain produces a sensation that becomes stronger as the body's need for water increases, motivating you to find something to drink. Heed that call, because once you feel thirst, you are already 2–3 percent dehydrated. When you have excess water, however, thirst is suppressed.

The other telltale sign of dehydration is the color of your urine. Pale yellow or "straw-colored" urine means you've been hydrating optimally. A brighter or more fully yellow urine is a signal that your kidneys are telling the body to retain water as it flushes out waste products—in other words, you're dehydrated. A darker yellow urine could also mean you've recently taken a bunch of supplements, including a megadose of vitamin C, which the body "pees out."

My last few hacks on water: Don't rely on your thirst to tell you that your body needs water, especially if you are middle-aged and older, because adults over fifty are more likely not to experience thirst in the same manner as younger people. (An app like Water Drink Reminder can be very helpful.)

Keep a bottle of water handy at your desk or nearby at home. Also, drink your water out of a Hydro Flask instead of a plastic bottle. If a plastic bottle warms up from sitting in a hot car or from being in the sun, toxins from the plastic can be released into your water. Not good for your health.

Last, because you're likely to wake up in a dehydrated state, drink at least twelve ounces of water first thing in the morning with a pinch of Himalayan sea salt, which contains trace amounts of calcium, potassium, and magnesium, and a splash of lemon juice, which helps alkalize the body. This is a great way to rehydrate first thing in the morning before you consume a coffee, eat breakfast, work out, or do anything else.

Cheers to you—and I hope to see you in the gym with your water bottle real soon!

BIG TIP #2: SUGAR IS THE DEVIL

Don't forget that I'm a recovering carb addict who grew up on plates of pasta and plenty of junk food in the 1970s and '80s. I'm talking about a diet heavy in pizza, spaghetti, ice cream, candy, and soda.

The standard American diet includes sugar-laden foods at every meal. There's breakfast with its sweet cereals; snack time with a Danish and coffee mixed with sugar; lunch with its soda, chips, and cookies; and dinner topped off with a variety of sweet, sugary desserts. Here's how much sugar we eat: according to the National Health Service, we consume an average of 152 pounds a year, or 3 pounds of sugar each week. That's like 42 teaspoons of sugar each day, which is absolutely crazy!

The trouble is that sugar's in nearly every commercially made food, from ketchup to salad dressing, from yogurt to barbecue sauce. Be wary of eating processed foods, meaning anything rolled off a production line or out of a commercial kitchen, because the manufacturers probably added sugar to make their product more palatable to the public.

Look at just about any food label these days and you'll find descriptions like corn syrup, high-fructose corn syrup, sucrose, corn sweeteners, sorghum syrup, fruit juice concentrate, and molasses. The healthier options are sweetened with honey, maple syrup, dehydrated cane juice, or unrefined sugar.

Food manufacturers know that we have a sweet tooth, and like everyone else, I have one as well. I can't tell you the number of times that I've wandered over to the pantry at 9:00 PM, just before bed, and started a conversation with a pouch of chocolate-covered almonds.

I know I'm dancing with the devil when that happens. If I let the conversation linger too long, the devil will win and I'll be thrown for a loss. Does anyone else know what I'm talking about?

I've had to get my mind right about dessert. Each time I stand in front of the pantry, I ask myself, *Do I really want this sweet snack? Do I need it?*

Of course, I don't *need* a handful of chocolate-covered almonds twenty minutes before I go to bed to survive the night. I sure *want* them, though, so I do my best to tell myself, *Todd, just suck it up. You aren't going to eat these right now.*

But those chocolate-covered almonds talk back, saying, *Just have a couple, then.*

This is where willpower has to come in, because you and I know the spirit is willing but the flesh is weak. We both know there's no way we can eat just one of those delicious morsels of chocolate. You have to willpower your way to the top with your mind right. If you win this battle, your next conversation with those chocolate-covered almonds will go much better.

164

Now, all this can be avoided by not buying treats like this in the first place, so be a careful shopper and stay away from store-bought cookies, muffins, cupcakes, ice cream, candy bars, and all those tempting treats you see at the checkout stand. You don't want to bring home those sweet impulse buys, because when cravings come along, and they will, the mind fights with the body, demanding, "I want my treat, and I want it now!" Stay on the perimeter of the grocery stores—where the produce, meat, and dairy sections are—and you'll be in much better shape.

I'm not saying you can't have any sugar. What I'm saying is that reducing your consumption of sweets will better sustain your energy, improve your overall health, and get your mind right.

BIG TIP #3: CONSUME MACROS IN YOUR DIET— PROTEIN, FAT, AND CARBS

There is so much confusion about "macros"—better known as protein, fat, and carbs—and what they are. Let me set the record straight and give you some guidelines to follow so you can amp up your health and vitality. Macros are your staple foods and must be taken seriously.

I'm not going to tell you the exact percentage of macros that you should eat, as I believe everyone is a bit different. What I will say is that by mastering my suggestions in this section, you will make significant improvement in your health and your overall performance.

1. Pound the protein. Proteins are the essential building blocks of the body and are required for the structure, function, and regulation of the body's cells, organs, tissues, and muscles. Protein generally comes from meat, fish, eggs, and dairy products, as well as from nuts, beans, and lentils. We need to eat protein because it provides for the transportation of nutrients, oxygen, and waste throughout the body.

Eating lots of high-protein foods like chicken, beef, dairy, and legumes slows the movement of food from the stomach to the intestine, which means you feel full longer and stave off hunger. Remember this about protein: if it once had a mom or a dad, it's probably good to eat. And the fewer legs, the better, meaning fish is better than chicken, and chicken is better than beef.

Protein builds muscle in the body and keeps us strong. When it comes to my recommendations for protein, I encourage most active men engaged in a serious training program to consume between .8 and 1 gram of protein per pound of body weight. So if you are a 200-pound male like me, you should consume 160 to 200 grams of protein per day.

Likewise, I advise most of my female clients looking to change body composition and get lean to consume between .6 and .8 grams of protein per pound of body weight per day. Therefore, a 150-pound female should consume between 90 grams and 120 grams of protein daily.

One more hack before I move on: if you are ever craving sugar during the day or longing for dessert, have a protein-filled snack instead. My go-to snack or dessert these days is chocolate almond milk with two scoops of protein powder. This "shake" works like magic to satiate my sugar cravings and provides me about 40 grams of protein in an instant.

2. Increase your consumption of healthy fats. The fats in many foods are good for us, providing a concentrated source of energy as well as the source material for cell membranes and various hormones. Furthermore, fats provide satiety. If there's no fat in the food, we'll be hungry within minutes of finishing a meal. We just have to eat the right fats.

Examples of some good fats to eat would be wild-caught fish, lamb, avocado, and cheese from organic sources, as well as nuts and nut spreads. "Bad fats" are the hydrogenated oils found in most packaged goods as well as margarine.

3. Trade in simple carbs for complex carbs. Carbohydrates come in two forms: simple and complex. Simple carbs—found in candy, sweet treats, fruit juices, sodas, and white and brown sugar—provide quick energy but lack a variety of vitamins, minerals, and fiber, which is why they are sometimes referred to as "empty calories." You also want to stay away from products made with refined white flour, like most commercial bread, bagels, and pasta—as well as breakfast cereals that are heavily sugared.

Complex carbohydrates, on the other hand, take longer to break down in the digestive tract because of their fiber and thus are better for you. Examples of complex carbohydrates would be foods like green, leafy vegetables; whole grains; oatmeal; bran cereal; brown rice; sweet potatoes; and pasta made from unrefined whole wheat. Oatmeal is my favorite breakfast and a great way to start the day.

The problem with carbohydrates is that we eat too many *refined* carbohydrates. Snacks have changed over the course of my lifetime. Kids once ate apples and oranges, but now they eat leather-like strips of fruit-flavored candy. Adults once ate a handful of raw almonds or cashews, but now they prefer honey-roasted peanuts, caked in sugar. Where fresh-squeezed orange juice was a breakfast staple, families now drink an artificially flavored orange drink, which is little more than orange soda, minus the bubbles.

The refining process strips grains, vegetables, and fruits of their vital fiber as well as their vitamin and mineral components. When you consume refined sugars and starches, they enter the bloodstream and spike a sudden increase in blood sugar. In response, the body's regulation mechanism kicks into high gear, flooding the bloodstream with insulin to bring blood sugar levels down to acceptable levels, which is why you "crash" after eating a blueberry muffin. Your body cannot cope with the spike in blood sugar levels.

Whenever possible, eat your carbohydrates fresh and unrefined. This includes copious amounts of fruits and vegetables, properly prepared grains, and small amounts of honey and other healthy sweeteners.

To provide you with a tangible number, my recommendation is to start with consuming at least five servings of fruits and vegetables per day. While it's recommended that you consume nine servings per day, most people are not even close to five. Start there.

Work on consuming more colored vegetables than fruit. A great goal to shoot for is three servings of vegetables and two servings of fruit. This will give you the vitamins, minerals, and fiber needed to keep you strong, healthy, and properly fueled for great health.

So dive into healthy fruits like strawberries, blueberries, black-berries, and apples, which are superfoods for your body and your brain. In addition, fortify your system with tons of vitamins, nu-trients, iron, and antioxidants from green leafy vegetables and colorful veggies. Spinach, kale, lettuce, celery, carrots, peppers, butternut squash, broccoli, and corn are all great examples of healthy vegetables.

If your diet consists primarily of lean sources of protein, healthy fats, and great sources of complex carbohydrates stemming from fruits and vegetables, you will undoubtedly be putting high-octane fuel in your system for peak performance. You'll be headed straight for the win.

BIG TIP #4: CONSIDER GOING GLUTEN-FREE TO GET RID OF BRAIN FOG AND BLOATING

I don't know what it's like in your part of the country, but in Southern California, restaurants know that they better have a few gluten-free options on the menu or they're going to see a big hit to their bottom line. Gluten-free diets are a big deal.

My consciousness has been raised about gluten, which is the general name for the proteins found in wheat, barley, and rye. Both Melanie and I have worked with naturopathic doctors and undergone allergy testing to see if gluten was an issue for us. Our results didn't show any official gluten intolerance, but there were plenty of times in recent years when I ate foods full of carbs and gluten—like my pasta—and felt bloated and heavy, like my insides were inflamed.

Melanie has experienced the same feelings of bloatedness, cramps, and abdominal pain as well as general lethargy. She decided to go gluten-free and hasn't looked back—she feels so much better. I'm still dancing with this gluten-free thing. Maybe I'll get there, but gluten is something I'm closely paying attention to because of the brain fog issue.

I mentioned brain fog earlier—memory loss, poor focus, and cloudy thinking. Thank goodness, I'm not dealing with these issues, but the number one topic I hear from my clients—at least those over forty years old—is that they feel like they've lost a step, so to speak, in the cognitive area. In other words, they have bouts of brain fog.

Brain fog is a symptom of gluten sensitivity, affecting up to 40 percent of gluten-intolerant individuals, according to a National Institutes of Health study. If you have symptoms like bloating, abdominal pain, diarrhea, constipation, or headaches after eating a meal rich in bread or pasta, then maybe you should get checked for an intolerance to gluten. Your best ally in the fight against brain fog may be a gluten-free diet.

BIG TIP #5: LET'S TALK ABOUT GETTING FAT

I'm sure you're thinking, *Wait a second, Todd. You already talked about fats in the macros section.*

I did. But I need to talk about fats again because they are that important.

Twenty-five years ago, the conventional wisdom was that anything with fat in it was bad for you, which led to a low-fat craze that swept the nation. Maybe you're old enough to remember those infomercials with platinum-haired Susan Powter screaming "Stop the insanity!" and "It's fat that's making you fat!" into the camera.

Suddenly, you could buy—and eat—cheese, crackers, cookies, yogurt, and ice cream with the magic words "fat-free" or "reduced fat" on the packaging. In a demonstration of the law of unintended consequences, fat-free foods did little for weight-conscious people except make them fatter because they thought they could eat more reduced-fat chocolate chip cookies than before.

We need to get our minds right about fat because "fats are bad for you" is a flat-out lie. Fats are our friends—as long as we consume the right types of fats. What are those? I mentioned earlier that some of the good fats to eat are found in organic milk and cheese, walnuts, and olives. Here are a few more:

• **Eggs.** We've come full circle on eggs, which got a bad rap a decade or so ago because of their high cholesterol levels. Eating foods high in cholesterol supposedly raised cholesterol levels in the blood. Eggs were high in cholesterol, which meant eggs were bad for the heart. Therefore, the medical community said no eggs.

These nutritional experts probably have a little egg on their faces now, because health experts have wised up to the benefits of eggs in recent years. They see eggs like I do: as a nutrient-dense food that packs six grams of protein, a bit of vitamin B_{12}, vitamin E, riboflavin, folic acid, calcium, zinc, iron, and essential fatty acids into a mere seventy-five calories. Here's another statement that will rock your world: eggs have the highest quality protein of any food, except for breast milk.

• **Avocados.** Avocado is a superfood with an abundance of enzymes, healthy fats, vitamin E, and fiber. I love avocado in my salad and smoothies and eating a whole avocado with a bit of lemon and dash of sea salt as a snack.

• **Coconut oil.** A great source of fat that's overlooked by many, coconut oil is packed with antioxidants and rich in vitamins E and K and the mineral iron. Coconut oil also contains medium-chain fatty acids (MCFAs) that are easily digested by the body and have been linked to health benefits like weight loss. Coconut oil performs well at high temperatures, so it's a great oil to use in a saucepan when sautéing vegetables or heating up leftovers. Coconut oil shows no signs of rancidity even after a year at room temperature.

• **Butter.** Even though I didn't know it at the time, I was onto something when I spread gobs of butter on my bread when I was a kid. Butter contains healthy saturated fats, especially butter produced from grass-fed cows. Butter is loaded with vitamins A, D, and E as well as other healthy nutrients. While butter is a healthy source of fat, you still can't eat unlimited amounts. I don't suggest spreading lots of butter on bread like I did when I was a kid.

• **Red meat from grass-fed cows.** Rich in iron and zinc and lower in fat, meat from grass-fed cows is generally leaner and far more nutritious than conventionally produced meat. Sure, organic, grass-fed meat is more expensive at the supermarket, but the health benefits *and* the superior taste will ensure your investment pays off from the very first bite. I've long believed that high-quality meat is worth the higher price. Remember, you are what you eat, and you don't want to be cheap when it comes to consuming protein.

• **Wild-caught fish and oily fish like sardines and mackerel.** Fish caught in the wild are a rich source of omega-3 fats, protein, potassium, vitamins, and minerals and should be consumed liberally. Farm-raised fish like salmon and tilapia do not compare to their cold-water cousins in terms of taste or nutritional value, however.

FOODS TO AVOID

What fats should you stay away from? Here's a short version of what is a very long list:

• **Foods fried in vegetable oil.** Sadly, too many people indulge their palates with deep-fried, high-calorie, high-sodium, high-sugar, and high-fat foods that they think taste good. Their taste buds have been manipulated by fast-food restaurants and food conglomerates that slap breaded coatings on chicken, sweeten meats with "secret sauces," and fry everything else.

• **Processed foods.** Breakfast cereals, potato chips, crackers, cookies, cake mixes, and other treats found in cupboards are all "creepers" that are devoid of nutrition and are loaded with sugar, saturated fat, trans fat, and usually high-fructose corn syrup.

• **Most desserts.** Ice cream, pies, parfaits, and cakes are problematic. The conversation I should be having with those chocolate-covered almonds is one sentence long: *My days of eating candy are over.*

These days, my desserts are typically the twelve to sixteen ounces of unsweetened chocolate almond milk along with one or two scoops of vanilla or chocolate protein powder. Or if I want to treat myself, I will take three tablespoons of full-fat Greek yogurt and add fruit, nuts, a scoop of almond butter, and a scoop of protein powder. After I mix it all up, I have a perfect—and healthy—dessert.

A final word about cravings. When I was pounding pasta and bread each night, I wasn't aware that my digestive system was breaking down all those carbs into sugar, which enters the blood. As blood sugar levels rise, the pancreas reacts quickly by producing insulin, a hormone that tells the cells to start absorbing blood

WHICH PROTEIN POWDER?

Protein powder has been the go-to "power snack" for me and my clients following a tough workout—or when cravings get the upper hand, which can happen if you ate excessive carbohydrates at your last meal. That's when you need to buffer all those carbs with a protein shake.

After a workout, I'm a fan of whey protein powder because it's a fast-digesting protein that quickly gets assimilated into your system. Whey protein is considered a complete protein because it contains all nine essential amino acids necessary for our dietary needs, and is low in lactose content. There are other protein powders made from egg, rice, hemp, and pea. Vegans can use protein powders made of brown rice, hemp, pea, and soy.

sugar for energy or storage. As our cells absorb more blood sugar, levels in the bloodstream begin to fall.

To compensate for this drop in blood sugar level, the body craves *more* carbohydrates. This is the body's attempt to maintain homeostasis, or an equilibrium, in blood sugar levels. That's not good if you're watching your weight. This is why it's important to consume more complex carbohydrate foods like whole grains (brown rice, oats, barley, and quinoa), legumes like lentils and chickpeas, and lots of fruits and vegetables, like apples, strawberries, pears, and prunes along with tomatoes, onions, beans, and zucchini.

Sure, fruits and vegetables have high levels of natural sugar, but they're a lot better for you than a handful of chocolate-covered almonds because they keep the body fueled for a long period of time and are also nutrient-rich as opposed to nutrient-empty. These complex carbohydrates often have lots of fiber, which bulks up stool, diminishes bloating and constipation, and reduces inflammation.

Now, I know what you might be thinking: *Hey, Todd, those fruits you mentioned. They're high in sugar, and we both know sugar is bad for you, so what do I do?*

Well, I've rarely worked with an overweight client in the gym who was trying to change body composition because they had eaten too much fruit over the years. Fruits do have sugar, but a handful of strawberries and blueberries on your oatmeal or in your protein shake—or grabbing an apple or a pear for an afternoon snack—are not the source of anyone's weight problem.

If you consumed all your sugar from fruit, you'd just benefit from the tremendous amount of vitamins, minerals, and antioxidants found in those foods. It's not the sugar from fruit that's making people fat or giving them brain fog.

Just make sure you're smart about how much fruit you eat and consume plenty of vegetables. When that happens, there's no way you're going to go wrong.

173

HOW MUCH FIBER DO YOU NEED?

A good rule of thumb is to consume 25 to 30 grams of fiber a day, which is around five times what most people get, so you'll likely have to be more proactive about getting more fiber in your diet. The best sources of fiber are fruits, vegetables, beans, and whole grains. The benefits of eating more fiber—or "roughage," as Grandma used to say—are many:

- You reduce inflammation.
- You improve your gut health because fiber binds to toxins and then you poop them out.
- You lower your cholesterol.
- You slow down glucose consumption.
- You help yourself lose weight.
- You lessen free-radical damage from fats.

Many fiber-rich foods contain two types of dietary fiber: soluble and insoluble. We need insoluble fiber because it's the kind that cleans out your colon like a broom, sweeping bacteria out of your intestinal tract. Did you know that you might have three to four pounds of stagnant bacteria in your gut? When things get blocked up down there, it's not good. Soluble fiber supports the good bacteria—known as probiotics—in your gut.

BIG TIP #6: SUPPLEMENT FOR SUCCESS

Here's how I feel about nutritional supplements—they should be supplementing an already healthy diet. I use the 90/10 rule: 90 percent of the time you want your diet to be on point. You can utilize help for that final 10 percent.

To make sure that you're getting the vitamins, minerals, and nutrients you need, I recommend taking supplements. Our foods aren't as nutritious as they used to be. Farming practices have changed a great deal since the 1950s. Today, pesticides are routinely sprayed on crops, and hormones are fed to cattle, chicken, and fish to fatten them up for the slaughterhouse or processing facility. That's why I'm a huge fan of going organic whenever possible, especially in purchasing grass-fed meat. In the long run, you're going to be happy investing in eating organic foods.

That said, I take supplements in the morning and in the evening. I'm not a pill popper per se; many of my supplements come in powder form, and the omega-3 fish oil I take comes right off the spoon, as a liquid.

There are many great vitamins, minerals, and multivitamins out there. Instead of mentioning them all, let me focus on the basic supplements I recommend if you're eating well, following a workout/training program, and looking for maximum health and recovery:

• **Glutamine.** This is the most abundant amino acid found in skeletal muscles. Glutamine is an essential amino acid, meaning that the body doesn't make it on its own. We must acquire glutamine from our food or from supplementation. Foods such as chicken, fish, cabbage, spinach, and dairy products are high in glutamine. I use a glutamine supplement found in powder form.

• **Branched-chain amino acids (BCAAs).** I know I'm getting technical here, but leucine, isoleucine, and valine are three BCAAs that have been shown to be ergogenic, or performance-enhancing. They increase focus and concentration to help get your mind right, burn fat, increase muscle mass, and reduce post-workout soreness. You get BCAAs primarily from beef, chicken, pork, fish, and shellfish, so if you don't eat meat, you should look at BCAA supplements.

• **Fish oil high in omega-3 fatty acids.** I like a tablespoon of Nordic Naturals Arctic Cod Liver Oil in the morning.

• **MCT oil.** Commonly extracted from coconut oil, MCT oil is high in omega-3 fatty acids as well, which supports brain health.

• **A good multivitamin.** Make sure you choose a multivitamin offering a wide range of vitamins and minerals, including vitamin D, zinc, and B-complex. Believe it or not, the best ones are prenatal vitamins.

• **Probiotics.** These supplements use lactobacillus or Bifidobacterium, which are good bacteria the gut needs.

• **Protein powder.** Consume two scoops of protein powder mixed with almond milk or water in the morning, after a workout, and one scoop at night if you've had a tough training day.

• **Beta-alanine.** If you take a pre-workout supplement like I do, there's a good chance that it has beta-alanine and caffeine in it. Caffeine is a well-documented ergogenic aid to boost energy and focus. Beta-alanine, on the other hand, is an amino acid that buffers lactic acid in the body, which builds up after intense bouts of exercise. Therefore, beta-alanine helps improve endurance, strength, power, and even recovery. I recommend 3.2 grams per day of beta-alanine. My preferred brand is CarnoSyn.

• **Creatine.** This would be a good place to say something about creatine, which is a popular supplement for improving performance in the gym and increasing muscle mass and strength. Five grams of creatine is the equivalent of five pounds of red meat, minus the fat and calories.

My athletes are constantly asking me whether they should have a creatine shake when we're done. I inform them that I do not recommend creatine for athletes under the age of eighteen, and for adults, I would only go so far as to recommend micronized creatine, which is better absorbed by the body.

Creatine works if you're looking to gain size and strength, but it can also dehydrate you, so increased hydration is needed, along with more attention and time on your flexibility routine.

LAST CALL

So there's some food for thought. Now it's up to you. Please think about what, how, and when you're eating, because good nutrition reduces the risk of developing chronic disease, positively affects your mood and mental health, and is a key part of getting your mind right.

These are all great reasons for eating foods as close to the natural source as possible. It's not cheap to invest in foods that contain the necessary nutrients to fuel and replenish our bodies, but it's better to pay the farmer now instead of the doctor later.

Adapt to a lifestyle where your food predicates your energy and performance. After all, let your food be thy medicine and let your medicine be thy food. It's time to eat to win!

Recovery Will Get Your Body and Your Mind Right

Life's a marathon, not a sprint.

—Phillip C. McGraw,
author of *Self Matters*

Maybe you don't recognize the author, Phillip C. McGraw, but I know you've heard of his alter ego—Dr. Phil, the host of the popular daytime show that tackles mental health issues.

Dr. Phil may have popularized the saying that "life is a marathon, not a sprint," but it's not original to him. The phrase reminds me of a discussion I had with Wayne Cotton around ten years ago. We were talking about my crazy, chaotic, and full-speed-ahead approach to work and my daily schedule when Wayne held up his hand.

"Todd, do you believe life is more like a marathon or a sprint?"

I didn't have to think two seconds to formulate an answer. "Of course, life is a marathon," I replied. "He who gets to the finish line first wins."

Was there any doubt that whoever ran the farthest faster than anyone else was always the winner? That's why I viewed life as the ultimate long-distance race: if I worked my tail off and stayed ahead of the pack, I'd get to the finish line before everyone else, which made me the winner . . . or so I thought.

Wayne set me straight. "You're absolutely dead wrong," he declared. "Life is not a marathon but a series of short sprints, followed by a time of recovery. Sprint. Recover. Sprint. Recover. I'm sure that's the same way you train your high-level pro athletes. You have them do a sprint, and then you give them a minute of rest. You train them for an hour or two, then you tell them to go get a massage. I know you factor in recovery time, which is why I'm concerned about *you*. From what I see, you need to emphasize more recovery in your lifestyle. Otherwise the rapid pace that you're running at will not only burn you out, but . . ."

Wayne stopped. I could tell he was thinking about what he wanted to say next.

"You'll end up dying early just like your father," he said softly.

I was stunned. My father was fifty-eight when he suffered a massive heart attack and died. That was awfully young, and I felt like he got robbed of some great living.

What Wayne said got me thinking about paying more attention to carving out downtime instead of cramming one more task and one more block of exercise into my jam-packed busy life.

For years I had been sprinting through life training athletes, managing a top-notch fitness facility, writing blogs for my website, creating YouTube videos, and hopscotching around the country and even the world to deliver high-energy keynote talks. Taking time off to reset and recharge? Why would I do that? I had always heard that if you love what you do, then you don't have to work a day in your life.

I never gave rest a thought until Wayne and I spoke that day more than ten years ago.

Since then, I have a whole new mindset about the importance of recovery on all levels—physically, mentally, emotionally, and energetically. From my exercise science background, I understood that strenuous exercise required intense effort, depleted energy sources, and could take a toll on muscles, joints, and tendons, so the body *had* to have time to recover.

I now view recovery as the yin to the yang of exercise, a necessary pause that replenishes the body's muscle glycogen (energy stores), repairs damaged tissues, and replaces fluid loss. If we don't allocate time to recover on a regular basis, then our workouts, our energy, and our relationships will suffer because we're not taking care of the most amazing machine ever designed—our bodies.

I don't think the topic of recovery gets enough attention. While most people intuitively comprehend that they should rest between sets of reps, they get caught up in the rat race and running like hamsters on a wheel when they are away from the gym.

There's no chance of getting their minds right. Their brains are not receiving nearly as much rest—in the form of sleep—as they need. This is why you need to be proactive about sleeping more as well as building in "mellow yellow" time so that you can recalibrate, rejuvenate, and re-energize your spirit, which will get your mind right in incredible ways.

MAKING TIME TO RECOVER

In the following sections, I'll be outlining my approach to recovery. Some of my ideas will sound familiar and come under a "best practices" umbrella, while others may come across as far-out. I'm not expecting you to adopt or even try every one of my notions, but I want you to be aware of what's out there, especially regarding the cutting-edge concepts I'm going to share.

You may have already picked up on this, but I'll say it anyway—I am a self-professed biohacker. If that's a new term for you, here's a simple definition: as a biohacker, I'm always looking for the latest, even avant-garde, approaches to training, performance, and recovery. Please know that biohacking is a positive term, and it has nothing to do with hacking computers. Biohackers follow their curiosity and investigate what science and technology are doing to make their bodies function more efficiently.

I've enjoyed researching and, yes, experimenting with every one of these recovery methods. Some of these ideas are inexpensive to incorporate, while others run a cost of thousands of dollars. Either way, I'm not expecting you to be an early adopter of these innovative recovery practices; I simply want to give you some wild ideas to chew on.

I'm constantly pushing the envelope of what I can do to look, feel, and perform my absolute best.

FIRST THINGS FIRST: GETTING A GOOD NIGHT'S SLEEP

Sleeping regularly and sleeping well is a great habit, but it's also a basic necessity. It's as fundamental to good health as air, food, and water. When you sleep well, you wake up feeling refreshed, revitalized—and ready to exercise. Dr. James B. Maas, author of *Power Sleep*, summed up the power of rest in this manner: "Sleep plays a major role in preparing the body and brain for an alert, productive, psychologically and physiologically healthy tomorrow."

When it comes to exercise and sleep, does a good night's rest give you more energy to exercise? Or does a well-rounded exercise program cause you to sleep better?

I'm sticking with the former, especially since I prefer to exercise in the early morning hours, long before I go to bed twelve to fourteen hours later. When I lay my head down on the pillow, a solid seven to eight hours of sleep is enough to allow my body the recovery it needs so I can wake up refreshed, do my quiet time, and then go after it in my home gym at 5:45 AM.

I understand that you may need seven, eight, or even nine hours of deep, undisturbed sleep, which sleep experts typically recommend. Whatever the amount of sleep you prefer, allow me to issue

MAKE SURE YOU GO TO SLEEP BEFORE MIDNIGHT

Are you a night owl?

I understand that you may be wired that way, but if you're a late-night person, make some sacrifices and fall asleep before midnight. One hour of sleep *before* midnight is more beneficial than several hours of sleep *after* midnight. I'm not sure why people have always said that, but I'm glad I'm usually dozing off to sleep by 10:00 PM. On the occasions when I've stayed up past midnight—like during the taping of the *Strong* episodes—I didn't feel well rested at all when I woke up in the morning.

I know my body: if I go to bed at 10:00 PM and get two hours of sleep before midnight, I'm going to be feeling great the next day.

a wakeup call about the importance of a good night's sleep. Rest rejuvenates the body and will make you as eager as me to attack the day with energetic gusto. When you get enough sleep, you're less vulnerable to sickness, accidents on the job or while driving the car, and depression.

The trouble is that sleep researchers tell us we have a "sleep gap," meaning that we don't sleep enough. While we all agree that sleep is as important to our health as exercising and eating right, too many of us aren't sleeping enough. The average American adult catches only 6.8 hours of sleep a night, according to a recent Gallup Poll, down more than an hour from 1942.

This is an incredibly unhealthy trend. If you don't get adequate sleep, then it's going to be very difficult to get your mind right as you start your day. A lack of sleep impacts your work performance and productivity and prevents you from thinking clearly. I've had business owners tell me about their sleep-starved employees going through the motions in their cubicles while work piles up, or how afternoon meetings drone on without resolve. And here's the biggest issue: when sleep-deprived workers say they are "too tired" to exercise at the end of the day.

Sleep remains a forgotten component of fitness and the number one element when it comes to recovery. If you're going to take getting your mind right seriously, then you need to be intentional about sleeping at least seven hours a night, or at least getting thirty to sixty minutes more sleep than you have been getting.

Sleep is an important part of your life—it's approximately one-third of your existence. Don't believe that you aren't doing anything while you sleep. The body has two big tasks to complete before you wake up:

1. Heal sore or damaged muscles. While you're sleeping, the body gets to work producing more white blood cells, which can attack viruses and bacteria seeking a foothold in your bloodstream. While you're asleep, the immune system fights harmful substances and the brain triggers the release of hormones that repair blood vessels and grow tissue.

2. Give the heart a break. When you're in sleep mode, the heart gets a chance to downshift and kick back for a while. Breathing slows, blood pressure drops, and inflammation is reduced.

When you wake up after a good night's rest, your hormones and stress levels have been adjusted for a more positive start to the day. There's a reason why you feel like you're getting a fresh start, and it's because the body was refreshed during eight hours of rest. Mentally, you're more prepared to face the challenges of a new day. Your mind is right.

Since we can all agree that sleeping well is great for our bodies and our minds, I know there are habits, which I described in Key #4, that prevent us from getting enough sleep: eating late; drinking caffeinated coffee and tea late in the day or at night; not "powering down" electronic devices; or plunking down in a La-Z-Boy and staying up to watch TV. When you watch television at bedtime, there's always one more favorite program to watch, one more news segment to view, and before you know it, it's way past eleven.

SPORTS AND THE DVR: A GREAT MIX

As a sports fan, I'm fortunate to live in the Pacific time zone because all the major sporting events start at five o'clock and end by nine. If you live in the eastern time zone, however, college football games, Sunday Night Football, Monday Night Football, the NBA playoffs, and World Series encounters will be problematic, since the evening games routinely end at midnight.

I recommend using your DVR to record your favorite sports for later viewing. Perhaps you can get up a bit earlier in the morning and watch the finish *real* quick before you go off to work or, if it's a weekend, before you open the morning newspaper or go online and find out who won.

Let today's technology work for you, not against you.

It's one thing to get seven to nine hours of sleep, but even more important than the *quantity* of sleep is enhancing the *quality* of sleep during the time you're actually resting. Here are some of my favorite ideas to improve your sleep quality:

• **Wear blue light glasses when looking at screens.** Laptops, smartphones, and tablets emit blue light, which leads to digital eye strain and sleep cycle disruption. If you've ever had itchy, dry, or red eyes after a long day staring at your computer, then you're a candidate for blue light glasses.

Blue light glasses are most useful at night when blue light disrupts your natural sleep patterns. If you absolutely must check out your Instagram account or catch up on emails after dinner, give blue light glasses a try. Studies suggest that continued exposure to blue light over time could lead to damaged retinal cells, according to the Prevent Blindness organization. The yellow- and orange-tinted lenses filter out the blue light so that you can lessen your exposure and reach REM sleep patterns more quickly.

• **Reach for the melatonin.** In Key #4, I touched on melatonin, which I use to help me sleep when I travel and change time zones, although I'll sometimes add a tablet of Tylenol PM when I fly to Europe. Here's another thing I do when I fly across the Pond: since transatlantic flights generally arrive in the early morning hours on the Continent, the first thing I do after arriving is work out. Breaking a sweat—and moving stiff muscles that sat a long time in a cramped economy seat—is a great way to get my mind right, especially if I'm trying to stay up all day to "reset" my body clock.

At night, I'll reach for melatonin, an all-natural supplement that comes in 1 mg, 3 mg, 5 mg, and 10 mg amounts. Medical professionals agree that melatonin, which is naturally produced in our bodies, is generally safe and doesn't cause a dependency, although some say there is a diminished response after repeated use. Side effects, if there are any, are headaches, dizziness, nausea, and a hangover feeling.

Based on your body weight, you'll probably want to try the 3 mg or 5 mg version, although you may find the 1 mg is enough to allow you to fall asleep in a timely manner. I think all of us can agree that it's no fun "counting sheep" and waiting for drowsiness to occur. If you have trouble sleeping, give melatonin a try.

• **Buy recovery bedding—and recovery pajamas while you're at it.** Did you know that you can purchase "recovery" bedsheets and pajamas? I didn't until I heard what my sponsor, Under Armour, was doing with New England Patriots quarterback Tom Brady.

Brady, a biohacker like me, heard something about "infrared clothing," which works along these lines: when heat from the body is absorbed into special "bio ceramic" particles located in a clothing pattern, then the heat is sent back to the body in the form of far infrared (FIR), which is a form of electromagnetic radiation that enhances circulation in the skin, modulates sleep, eases aches and pains, and reduces inflammation. Brady and Under Armour even teamed up to produce a line of "athletic recovery sleepwear" a few years ago.

Brady, the first NFL quarterback to win five Super Bowls, told a *Boston Globe* reporter, "Sleep is something that I have talked about for many years now, how important it is to recovery, not just for athletes but for everybody." After noting that he sleeps between eight and nine hours a night, Brady said, "That's the only way for me. I'm forty-two, and I'm still playing with these kids, so I've got to get as much rest as possible."

UA's athletic recovery sleepwear comes in short- and long-sleeve tops and pants and shorts and isn't cheap—between $120 and $150 for a set. The interiors of the garments are covered in a hexagonal ceramic mineral print that absorbs the heat that the body radiates and reflects far infrared back to the skin.

I started wearing UA's recovery sleepwear after my partial knee replacement in late 2018. I've also worn the sleepwear bottoms under my sweatpants on long plane flights to promote blood circulation, prevent swelling of the legs, and help guard against deep vein thrombosis (DVT), much like compression socks do.

So, Todd, do these fancy "performance pajamas" work?

Quick answer: they certainly haven't hurt. I do feel like I've woken up with fresh legs and feeling good. Under Armour points to a scientific study in *Photonics Lasers*, a medical journal, done at Massachusetts General Hospital and Harvard's Department of Dermatology, showing that the recovery pajamas increased blood flow, which helps the muscles. Michael Hamblin, one of the researchers, said, "I'm pretty sure there is some effect. I wouldn't call it a dramatic effect." That's likely a fair assessment.

Meanwhile, Under Armour has a whole stable of athletes sleeping in the recovery sleepwear, including baseball slugger Bryce Harper, ballerina Misty Copeland, a bunch of college basketball teams, and the Southampton soccer team in the English Premier league.

They're also sleeping on Under Armour's athletic recovery bedding, which is the same bedding Melanie and I have on our king-size bed. I got the recovery bedding sheets right before my knee surgery. I wasn't going to leave any stone unturned. While the jury is still out, I like how I'm feeling when my body stirs each morning right on time—5:00 AM.

After all, when it comes to sleep, I'm not messing around!

• **Look to aromatherapy to relax the body.** French chemist René-Maurice Gattefossé coined the term *aromatherapy* nearly a century ago when he used lavender oil to heal his burned hands. Lavender oil is one of many essential oils taken from plants, flowers, shrubs, trees, bushes, and seeds that are used in healing ways.

I like to put a bit of lavender oil in an essential oil diffuser on my nightstand when I fall asleep. Lavender has a wonderful smell that helps relax the brain, and I'll sometimes spray a bit on my pillow if I've had a particularly stressful day.

If you're the type who likes to take a bath before going to sleep, several drops of lavender in the water is a great idea. But if you're really looking to recover from a tough workout, a steep hike, or a long day in the saddle, then I recommend a hot bath with lots of Epsom salts. For most people, there's something very therapeutic about water, especially hot bath water scented with lavender and a handful of Epsom salts.

That said, I'm not a bath person. Melanie loves her Epsom salt baths and assures me that a warm bath does wonders for soothing the soul, which doesn't surprise me. Aromatherapy, which has been around in some form since the days of the Egyptian pyramids, relaxes the mind in incredible ways and calms you down for a good night's sleep.

• **Install blackout shades.** Your bedroom should be dark when you sleep. If light from the next-door-neighbor's porch or moonlight seeps through the windows, consider installing blackout curtains, shades, and blinds to cut the amount of light entering the bedroom. They're worth the investment.

• **Wear a sleeping mask.** If installing blackout curtains is not possible or practical, then consider using a sleeping mask. You can also don a sleeping mask at daybreak if you need an extra hour of shut-eye.

• **Get a sound machine.** There are dozens of different sound machines that create ambient white noise to drown out background noises and lull you into a deeper rest. You can choose from basic white noise to soothing sounds from nature, like ocean waves, falling rain, or the sound of night crickets.

A sound machine can put you into a state of relaxation that induces your parasympathetic nervous system—also known as the rest-and-digest system—to regulate your heart rate and blood pressure while increasing intestinal activity.

• **Go for a "power nap."** Sometimes referred to as the "pastor's secret," the old-fashioned power nap—defined as ten to twenty minutes of sleep and rest during the workday—can significantly improve alertness and job performance. One study found that midday naps taken by medical residents, who often put in exhausting twenty-four-hour shifts, improved their cognitive functioning and alertness, which resulted in a 30 percent decrease in attention failures. Getting enough rest is not only good for your health, it's also a great career move. A study in the medical journal *Behavioural Brain Research* found that naps are better than caffeine for improving verbal memory, motor skills, and perceptual learning.

It used to be that only little children and old folks took naps, but big companies like Google, Samsung, Huffington Post, and Zappos are waking up to the importance of sawing some z's in the middle of the afternoon. These companies provide nap facilities— "safe zones" if you will—where employees can sleep on the job and return to work recharged, more alert, and primed for productivity. Some companies have introduced EnergyPods, a futuristic-looking chair with an eggshell hood that creates a zero-gravity sleeping position. I've never tried one, but the reviews from users are positive.

GOING BEYOND SLEEP FOR BETTER RECOVERY

Sleep is the most important aspect of recovery. Without enough rest, you can't function optimally. But beyond sleep, there are many other modalities and techniques that can help you recover and rejuvenate the body, mind, and soul. Here are several of my favorite

189

methods that I use to optimize recovery and increase overall health, vitality, and performance.

• **Get a soothing massage or go for more intense bodywork.** There's no doubt that a relaxing massage feels incredible, helps muscles recover faster, and reduces pain throughout the body. I've been the beneficiary of hundreds of massages over the years and have *given* thousands of massages, so I have a pretty good handle on what massage therapy can do.

My undergraduate coursework in kinesiology at The College of William & Mary gave me my first understanding of the body's physiology. After graduation, I pursued my dream of playing in the NFL by living in Europe, flinging passes in the minor leagues of pro football. During my first off-season, I got certified as a massage therapist at what was then New Life Institute in Atlanta. My plan was to earn a good hourly rate working on other people's aching muscles while continuing to train my body for the upcoming football season. While at the New Life Institute, I also learned about Rolfing, Feldenkrais, myofascial release, and integrative bodywork techniques.

A few years later, my back got majorly wrenched while playing football in France. I limped home to New Jersey and stayed with my oldest sister, Patti, who owned a day spa, Therapeutic Touch, in Bay Head. After receiving treatment on my back, I'd hang out at the spa since I didn't have much to do. One afternoon, a woman named Jenna King introduced herself and said she heard I was a heck of an athlete who knew something about massage therapy.

"Would you be available to do any bodywork?" she asked.

I was an unemployed twenty-five-year-old broken-down quarterback with limited experience in massage therapy, but if someone wanted to pay me to work with my newfound skill set until I figured out what to do in life, I was game.

"Sure, I can do that," I heard myself saying.

And that's how I was introduced to Jenna's husband, Michael King, the weekend warrior with a bad back and CEO of King

World Productions, who I mentioned in Key #1. Since Michael maintained homes on both coasts, he persuaded me to move to Los Angeles so I could continue to work with him as a personal trainer and do bodywork and massage on his beat-up body.

What's the difference between massage therapy and bodywork? One generally chooses massage for therapeutic reasons—to warm up muscle tissue and release tension. Most people have heard of Swedish massage, a relaxing technique accomplished by rubbing the muscles with long gliding strokes that sends blood in the direction of the heart. Swedish massage is fairly gentle on the body and is the most common type of massage performed in the US.

I'm not one of those Swedish massage guys who likes a light rubdown with a scented candle. Nothing wrong with that, but I prefer a substantially deeper massage where the muscles really feel it. I refer to this type of massage as "bodywork" because it's much more intense. Bodywork breaks down muscle knots and adhered tissues, also known as adhesions, while addressing specific areas of muscle pain, stiffness in the back, poor posture, and a lack of flexibility and mobility.

I describe the difference like this: Pretend that you take your used car to a body shop one day. If you're looking to have the car detailed to a shiny polish, that would be like getting a Swedish massage. But if you're looking for something more substantial, like punching out a body panel and filling in door dings so that your car is restored to tip-top condition again, that would be bodywork.

I enjoy receiving a therapeutic Swedish massage every now and then, and a relaxing massage can help with any recovery plan. But you're always going to get a bit more bang for your buck with bodywork and its heightened physical manipulation of damaged, tired muscles and compromised soft tissues.

So the next time you book a massage, ask what type you're going to be receiving. Or pose the question, "Do you do bodywork?"

Because a deep-tissue massage is what you really should be after.

• **Check out percussive therapy from a massage gun.** If you're a member of a first-rate gym, studio, or club, you've probably noticed the personal trainers using a lightweight, battery-operated muscle treatment device, known as a "massage gun," on clients' glutes, legs, shoulders, and back muscles. The massage gun I use is a Theragun, which produces forty vibrations per second and looks like a mini-jackhammer. It has a sponge-like prong or rubber mallet that turns your muscles into jelly with "percussive therapy."

I bought my first Theragun when I was doing *Strong*, the NBC reality show, and it really helped me get through the competitions. You place the massage knob on a sore muscle or pressure point, hit the On button, and receive a tremendous massage in a short amount of time.

A Theragun or similar percussion device generally runs from $300 to $600. You can use one on yourself, but you're limited by your reach to your arms, legs, and hips. If you have a kink in your back, for instance, you'll have to ask a spouse, partner, or friend to massage you because you can't reach the upper and lower back and shoulder muscles by yourself.

I use my Theragun most days of the week before a workout or at night before I go to sleep. It feels great, and I'm grateful that percussive therapy is now part of my overall self-care routine.

• **Tired legs? Then check out NormaTec.** They look like the pads that ice hockey goalies wear when they patrol the net, but compression boots, as they are called, help your legs after an intense workout by aiding the body in transporting excess fluid out of the limbs. They're portable and can be used at home. All you have to do is slip them on your legs while sitting in a chair or recliner or while lying in bed and then relax.

As the attachments fill with compressed air, they mold themselves to the user's exact shape. Then the system begins applying compression, followed by pulsing, holding, and releasing. Each section of the legs receives crucial pressure to keep fluid moving toward the body's core.

There are several different kinds of compression boots on the market, but the highest-rated ones are produced by NormaTec, which utilizes a pulse technology versus a more conventional squeezing motion to aid in your recovery.

I started using NormaTec compression boots during the taping of *Strong* and felt they did so much for me that I purchased my own pair. (Cost is around $1,500.) These days, even my kids use them.

You can also get recovery systems for your hips and your upper body. A number of my quarterbacks and pitchers use NormaTec sleeves on their million-dollar arms. I love this pulsing technology and what it does for recovery, and so do my athletes.

• **If you really want to shake things up, book a session in a float tank.** Consider this:

It's pitch black around me. I can't see or hear anything as I float faceup in a foot of water mixed with a thousand pounds of Epsom salts, inside a lightproof and soundproof tank that's the size of a twin bed. The air and the water are the same temperature as my body's skin—between 93 and 95 degrees Fahrenheit—so it's difficult to know where my body ends and where my surroundings begin.

I'm floating like a cork because the amount of Epsom salts in the warm-but-not-hot water makes the water ten times more buoyant than the ocean. I'm able to float effortlessly on the surface with my face comfortably above the water, an effect similar to the weightlessness that astronauts feel when they're in space. Not only is it great for my body to experience near weightlessness, but the calming experience allows my mind to reach a near meditative state.

After a short time—three minutes? ten minutes?—I mentally let go. There are zero distractions on my mind. Any tension in my muscles is practically gone. I'm floating in an environment that feels like zero gravity, which is an odd sensation, but it feels oh-so-good. My spine naturally strengthens and lengthens, and my brainwaves enter a state similar to a deep sleep cycle. My mind is getting more right by the minute as I drift off to a faraway place totally devoid of all senses.

What I've described is a "flotation therapy" session at Livkraft Performance Wellness in La Jolla, a coastal town north of downtown San Diego. A friend of mine, Pete Tobiason, owns this flotation therapy storefront, where clients book sixty- to ninety-minute sessions. I wish I could float more often than I do.

Before my first hour-long session, I was told that the enclosed environment could be claustrophobic, but I had no issues. I was totally comfortable in there, with 180 gallons of warm water and nearly a half-ton of Epsom salts, which remove toxins and lactic acids from muscles. Using a float tank shortens recovery time considerably and will allow you to return to the sport or activity you love the most. The weightless environment allows the muscles and joints to relax, which increases blood flow and circulation.

I've found float therapy to be a highly effective and super enjoyable experience. Float tanks are generally located on the East and West Coasts, so if you live in the Midwest, you might have trouble finding a facility close to home. But if you happen to vacation in a major metropolis on either coast, treat yourself to an hour-long session.

You'll be as amazed as I was.

• **To go to the next level in recovery, think hyperbaric.** I train a number of elite athletes who use hyperbaric oxygen therapy to overcome an injury or speed up their recovery from the smashing hits they take on the football field. With hyperbaric therapy, an NFL running back might recover in four days instead of eight, or a lineman with a bruised thigh could mend in one week, not three. Thanks to the significant reduction in recovery time, hyperbaric oxygen therapy is popular among injured professional athletes trying to get back into the game.

At the start of therapy, the athlete slides into a portable hyperbaric chamber, which is gradually pressurized with pure oxygen until it reaches twice the normal atmospheric pressure. This allows the greater absorption of oxygen throughout the body's tissues. The process gives up to a tenfold increase in the oxygen level of blood plasma and hemoglobin. The athlete is reminded to relax and breathe normally during treatment and may experience ear popping or mild discomfort, but that usually disappears if the pressure is lowered a bit.

Hyperbaric chambers in a hospital setting cost well more than $100,000, while portable versions for home use are considerably cheaper at less than $5,000. In hospital settings, hyperbaric chambers are generally used for patients who have experienced heart failure or are dealing with slow-healing wounds. Placing cardiovascular patients in a hyperbaric chamber accelerates recovery. Only half the amount of time is required for a patient's heart to resume normal electrical activity.

As for portable chambers, they operate at a lower pressure than hospital-grade hyperbaric ones, which makes them safer while providing many of the same medical benefits as higher-pressurized chambers.

Another version of hyperbaric therapy is when a hyperbaric tent is hooked up to the back end of an oxygen generator and set up inside a home or enclosed around a bed. Also known as an altitude-simulation tent, you can duplicate high-altitude training by sleeping in a hyperbaric tent overnight.

Some of my athletes have installed a hyperbaric tent in their homes and use it to replicate training in high elevations. From listening to their enthusiasm, this recovery treatment definitely deserves to be part of the mix.

The ability of hyperbaric therapy to increase the volume of oxygen in the blood is what draws top athletes to go to the effort—and expense—of overcoming injury or flushing out lactic acid that causes muscle fatigue. I've tried hyperbaric therapy because I needed to know if this form of treatment is something I can recommend to my professional and collegiate athletes. After experiencing hyperbaric oxygen therapy and witnessing how this treatment has helped my athletes, I can give this treatment protocol a thumbs-up.

• **Don't give a cold shoulder to cryotherapy.** At the 2019 French Open in Paris, the players who came off the court after grueling four-hour matches on the red clay of Roland-Garros had a new recovery therapy to test. I'm referring to cryotherapy, a treatment that involves standing in freezing-cold temperatures—I mean really cold, as in minus 220 degrees Fahrenheit—for a short time.

The athletes say it really works, which is why cryotherapy is being called the hottest thing—well, maybe that isn't the greatest word choice—to help the body recover while reducing the risk of injury, promoting sleep, and raising energy levels.

The players strip down to their underwear; put a mask on to cover their mouths; don a wool ski cap to cover the head and ears; wear oversized gloves, socks, and slippers; and step into a pair of chambers, each the size of a shower stall.

The protocol is to stand in the first chamber, which is set at minus 76 degrees Fahrenheit. The duration is only twenty seconds, but that's just a warm-up. The next move is to step inside a second chamber, where the temperature has been dialed down to an incredibly numb minus 166 degrees Fahrenheit or even minus 220 degrees Fahrenheit.

Athletes remain inside the second chamber for up to three minutes, if they can hack the extreme cold. Some panic and pull the rip cord because they want out, but those who cope are generally rewarded with less muscle soreness and a good night's sleep. Top players like Rafael Nadal, Roger Federer, Stan Wawrinka, and Alexander Zverev have become instant fans of cryotherapy.

I *had* to try cryotherapy after hearing about it from some of the NFL athletes I train. Instead of entering cryotherapy stalls, these players stand inside a circular chamber that allows them to leave their head exposed while freezing temperatures surround them from the shoulders down. Although it's not complete immersion in the cold, the effect is nearly the same: healed muscle tissues and sped-up recovery from injuries.

I've now stood in a cryotherapy chamber dozens of times, resetting my body's core temperature and experiencing a deep cellular level of healing. Each session generally lasted three minutes, and I was *cold* when my time was up. But I knew my body had just received a jump start on Recovery Road.

I'm such a fan of cryotherapy that I have a mobile cryotherapy company visit Fitness Quest 10 every few months. You should see the line out the door when the van pulls up. Cost? Fifty dollars for a three-minute session.

A cheaper version of cryotherapy is the ice bath, which has been around for ages. I grew up with ice baths in the locker room after football games and am still a big believer in them. These days, I live next to the largest ice bath in the world—the Pacific Ocean. The ocean temperature hovers in the high 50s from October to May, which I know is considered warm in many wintry parts of the world. Still, a three-minute "polar bear" plunge can be quite invigorating.

• **At the opposite extreme of ice-cold therapy are infrared saunas.** You have probably sat in a traditional sauna, broiling like a lobster, the air around you hotter than 150 degrees Fahrenheit.

I prefer infrared saunas, which have panels that use electromagnetic radiation to produce heat rays somewhere between 120 degrees and 160 degrees Fahrenheit. Whereas the heat from a traditional "dry" sauna is only topical, infrared heat waves penetrate deeper into the body, up to an inch or more under the skin, which can accelerate the recovery of tired and sore muscles and joints. The temperature of the body's core increases, not just the temperature of the skin surface, which is the case with a traditional sauna. The body also sweats a lot more with infrared saunas, which releases more toxins, increases blood flow, and boosts cardiovascular circulation.

When I expanded Fitness Quest 10 in 2006, I made sure we added an infrared sauna to our facility. It was such a hit with our clients that I've added a second one.

RANKING THE RECOVERY METHODS

How would I rank all these recovery methods? Let me prioritize them in this order, on a scale of 1 to 10, with 10 being best:

- I'd rate massage and bodywork a 10. When a skilled expert manually manipulates muscle and fascia, there's nothing better for your mind, body, and recovery.
- I'd say that a percussive massager like a Theragun is a 9, and it's an economical recovery tool. All coaches and trainers should have a massage gun as part of their arsenal for their clients.
- Infrared saunas are a solid 8, as are NormaTec compression sleeves for the legs and arms.
- I'm going to rank hyperbaric chambers and cryotherapy at a 7 or 8. They certainly work, but these treatments are expensive. Ice baths do the job for a fraction of the price.
- Flotation therapy is super relaxing and a wonderful way to spend an hour, but it's like a Swedish massage—it feels good at the time but is not long lasting. I'd rank it a 6 or a 7.

STEM-CELL THERAPY: THE FUTURE OF RECOVERY?

I can't resist bringing up one last recovery method. You'll be hearing more about it as the technology develops. I'm referring to stem-cell therapy, or to be precise, cell-free therapy (CFT), an amazing method I got a chance to try recently.

This type of therapy uses secretions of your own stem cells—known as extracellular vesicles (EVs) and taken from one's body fat—to repair and regenerate damaged tissue. Sometimes called "master cells" or the body's "raw material," stem cells are what the body uses to make blood, grow bones, and develop the brain and the body's organs.

Conventional wisdom was that stem cells did all the work, but being the biohacker I am, I've discovered that's already outdated—that it's really the EVs (so tiny they even get through the blood-brain barrier to help neurodegenerative conditions) that are the agents of repair and regeneration. If you get enough of your own EVs reintroduced by simple infusion, amazing things start to happen.

I've experienced CFT myself with a unique medical advisory group in Europe. I received approximately 10 billion of my own EVs, which is far more effective than a few hundred thousand one may get with a typical stem-cell transplant. CFT is also safer than stem-cell transplants: you receive only your own EVs, so there's no risk of adverse reactions. The ethical issues with embryonic stem cells aren't even part of the picture. Additionally, the IV infusion into the bloodstream has proven to be more effective and often has ancillary benefits.

The science behind stem cells is complex and belongs in the "new frontier" category, but the potential is exciting for those with muscular/skeletal damage (new or old) from sports injuries and a host of other medical conditions.

The problem with whole stem cells is highlighted by the US Food and Drug Administration (FDA), which has approved only a very limited number of stem-cell therapies, mainly involving the production of bone marrow for transplants in cancer care and cord blood for specific blood-related disorders. There are no approved stem-cell treatments for other diseases at this time.

Right about now, you may be thinking, *Isn't stem-cell therapy banned, like taking a performance-enhancing drug (PED)?*

The answer is no. In fact, many sporting organizations governing professional sports have cleared the use of stem cells and CFT as part of an injury repair program. This form of "regenerative medicine" using concentrated EVs can strengthen and accelerate recovery dramatically but, as I just mentioned, these treatments have not yet been approved by the FDA.

This means that those seeking CFT must travel to Europe (or Bermuda) for "experimental treatment" on an individual basis. Nonetheless, many NFL and NHL players have flown to Europe in the last decade seeking CFT, including quarterback Peyton Manning, who returned to the playing field to win the Super Bowl again in 2016 after receiving CFT treatment. Generally, NFL and NHL teams won't pick up the tab, so the players foot the cost of this expensive procedure. If CFT accelerates your recovery, reduces the risk of future injury, and extends your playing career, then I'd say it's a sound investment.

Following my partial knee replacement surgery in late 2018, I looked into cell-free therapy as a way to aid the recovery of my right knee. But there was another reason lurking in my mind: the concussions I received while playing football in high school and at the college and professional level. I can count at least six times when I had my "bell rung," as we used to say on the football field.

Because I thought that my EVs could make a difference regarding my knee recovery as well as the health of my brain, I decided to go for it in the spring of 2019. In the US, I had a little fat taken via a procedure that mimicked liposuction. The fat cells were then sent by medical courier to labs in Europe, where they were harvested. Four weeks later, my 10 billion EVs were ready for a simple IV infusion. I took a quick trip to Europe, and everything was done in one of the least intrusive procedures you can imagine.

I had read research stating that EVs travel everywhere in the body, not just to those areas of your body crying the loudest. My brain and my right knee were important, sure, but it was the state of my mind that propelled me to pay for the trip. Anything to get my mind right, yes?

I've been following the stories about CTE in recent years, like many of us who played football. If you've seen the movie *Concussion* starring Will Smith, then you're aware of chronic traumatic encephalopathy (CTE), which is a progressive, degenerative disease of the brain found in people with a history of repetitive brain trauma—like those who played football.

EVs have the ability to repair damaged brain cells (hence the success with neurodegenerative conditions like multiple sclerosis and Parkinson's). A biohacker like me will go to the extremes and the expense to buy myself not only more time but a better quality of life.

I've experienced a half-dozen concussions—and sprained and strained nearly every joint, ligament, and muscle in my body—so I'm doing everything I can in my late forties to make sure that I feel my best, perform at the highest level, and always think clearly and with focus. If CFT can help the quality of my brain, then I'm going for it. I want to think straight and think big.

So that's my foray into the world of cell-free therapy, which has some twenty-five years of research data behind it in government-approved labs. If this treatment helps my brain stave off potential onset dementia and allows me to make a full recovery on my right knee, then it will all be worth it.

Let me ask you this as I come to the end of this important chapter: What is your health worth? What avenues are you willing to follow to fortify your body and mind?

I can't answer that for you, but I urge you to give this topic of recovery some serious thought.

It might just get your mind right—and it will definitely get your body right!

FOURTH QUARTER

FINISHING STRONG

If you're going to be a champion in sports, business, or life, you always have to finish strong. I often say that good players can speed a game up, and the great ones can slow a game down. At the end of the fourth quarter or the end of the game, the best in the world know what it takes to get the job done.

Is it time for you to "speed up" or "slow down"? Either way, it's time for you to step up and finish strong.

KEY #9

Tap Into the Whispers

In all your ways acknowledge Him,
and He will make your paths straight.
—Proverbs 3:6 BSB

You probably know by now that I'm not the type of guy who likes to plop down on a couch, grab the remote, and spend hours watching mindless TV shows—although I do love watching football on TV.

So consider my mindset when I came home from the hospital following my partial knee replacement surgery in November 2018. What was I going to do with myself? I knew that for the next five or six weeks I was under house arrest—doctor's orders. I couldn't drop in at Fitness Quest 10 to see how everyone was doing. I couldn't go shopping for groceries. I couldn't even watch my kids' sporting events. My job was to limit my movement and let the body do what it does best—rest, heal, and recover from a major surgery.

As this new reality set in, I thought about how I could get my mind right during this new chapter in my life. I was thinking . . .

thinking . . . when I had a eureka moment: *Dude, you're on sabbatical!*

Sabbatical was the right word to describe this compulsory break from my normal routine. I'd never taken a long break like this in my life, but the more I thought about it, recuperating from surgery on my right knee afforded me a priceless opportunity to contemplate where I stood in life as well as recharge my mental batteries.

I decided that I would make the most of my enforced time off. Instead of spending just fifteen minutes reading my Bible and praying, like I usually did between five and six in the morning, I had an hour . . . or two—or as long as I wanted.

This huge chunk of time gave me the chance to study Scripture and go deeper in my faith than ever before. I *wanted* to utilize these five to six weeks of healing as a time to go deeper in my own faith. This sort of thinking really got my mind right.

Just eleven months earlier, I'd stated in my 2018 Annual Roadmap & Strategic Plan that I wanted to take a four-to-eight-week sabbatical in the mountains. Well, sure enough, I was getting my sabbatical. It wasn't in the mountains, but this break from life would allow me to do what I needed and wanted to do: quiet the mind, write, pray, journal, and just be still so that I could "tap into the whispers."

So here's what I did while Melanie was teaching at Southwestern College and the three kids were in school: Sitting in my recliner, with a Game Ready ice machine providing cold compression around my right knee, I'd read my Bible and a devotional book for about an hour. When I reached a stopping point, I'd pick up my journal on my end table, and I would just sit still. There was no TV on. There was no radio on. The house was completely quiet.

I'd place the journal in my lap and hold a pen in my hand. Then I'd *listen* to whatever came into my head, ready to write down what I heard God say to me. I wanted to hear God whisper into my heart. I wanted to ignore the shouts in my head like, *You need to do this, Todd!* or *You better take action or you're going to miss out!*

Midway through my recuperation, I heard these whispers:

- *You must give up good to get to great.*
- *Success traps are harder to get out of than failure traps.*
- *You must trust Me. TRUST Me.*
- *It's time for change. Put your faith completely in Me.*

The whispers were getting louder and louder each day and with every passing week. I continued to hear the same messages in my mind.

You may not know the context of what God was saying to me, but I sure did: it was time to execute the greatest organizational staff changes that I'd ever made in my nearly twenty-year career at my gym. If I was going to go from good to great, if I was going to have an impact beyond the walls of Fitness Quest 10, that meant delegating responsibilities so I'd be free to speak more often around the country, start my own podcast, meet more people at trade show conventions, become a valued resource at corporate retreats, and yes, even write more books.

It was one thing to contemplate what needed to be done and another to release and let go of my hesitations and fears. As I tapped into the whispers day after day, I heard God repeat the same thoughts about going from good to great, about getting out of success traps, and about trusting Him. I kept hearing that word *trust* every day. That's when I realized that I needed to pull the trigger and make some important changes in my life.

Without getting into the particulars of everything I did, my biggest move was elevating Julie Wilcox, who'd been my general manager at Fitness Quest 10 for more than a decade, to the role of Director of Global Development for Todd Durkin Enterprises. In essence, I replaced myself. Julie would now spearhead initiatives

THE POWER OF JOURNALING: A GREAT WAY TO TAP INTO THE WHISPERS

I'm not one of those guys who easily sits still and can meditate for long stretches of time. That's not how I tap into the whispers.

Where it all starts for me is journaling. This time of introspection jump-starts everything. Typically, when I start journaling, there are competing voices in my head: some shouting, some whispering. I key in on the whispers with the quiet faith that it's the Spirit speaking to me. He could ask me to write something down that I'm grateful for, which would remind me of the virtue of gratitude. He could ask me to outline a delicate discussion I need to have with a teammate or employee. He could say to me, *You need to share this on social media today.*

I try to tap into all these whispers because I'm trying to live with purpose. When I hear Him ask me, *Are you living for Me or living for yourself?* then I know He wants me to differentiate between my agenda and my divine purpose.

If there's one thing I've learned over the years of seeking to hear God's voice, it's this: when I tap into the whispers and am obedient to what I hear, great things are going to happen.

and opportunities that I didn't have time to get to because of everything else I had going on.

Stepping into Julie's former role as GM would be Jeff Bristol, who would become responsible for the day-to-day operations at Fitness Quest 10. Lisa Evanovich would graduate from being the head of our "Directors of First Impressions" to becoming the new assistant GM. Additionally, I named Frank Pucher as director of the Todd Durkin Mastermind Group, which gave Larry Indiviglia an even greater leadership role inside Todd Durkin Enterprises.

Julie, Jeff, Lisa, Frank, and Larry were extremely excited about their new responsibilities, and they've done a great job taking the reins of Todd Durkin Enterprises and Fitness Quest 10, freeing me up to pursue some incredible opportunities. But I wouldn't have made this move unless I had tapped into the whispers during prayer time. This is why I urge you to find a quiet time, read Scripture, pray, and then ask God to speak into your heart.

Tap into the whispers.

You'll be glad you did.

HEARING FROM HIM

I'd say that 95 percent of the time when I speak, I'm talking to a secular audience. I have no problem with that. That's my norm. I'm a coach at heart who wants to impact others to improve their fitness level, get their minds right, and live longer, happier lives. I'm not a pastor like Dr. Jeremiah or Miles McPherson of the Rock Church in San Diego, where we regularly attend.

When I am introduced to a corporate audience or a roomful of fitness club owners and managers, I understand that they're not expecting to hear a lot of God talk. So when I get to the part where I describe the importance of having a quiet time before starting your day—a period of being introspective and reading something inspirational—I counsel my audience to "tap into the whispers." I do that because I want them to open their minds and their hearts to hearing from God.

Some will have ears to hear, and others won't.

Listen, I'm not here to judge. My mission is to motivate and inspire people to greatness and create impact every day. My hope is that when my time is up, I have used my gifts to impact 10 million people to live a life worth telling a story about. That's my mission. But if you've made it this far into *Get Your Mind Right*, maybe you're interested in why I'm so invested in my relationship with God.

I told you that I was raised in an Irish-Catholic home. Mom made sure we were in the pews every Sunday morning for Mass, especially after Dad left us. When he came back into my life when I was ten, my interest in God and church kicked up a notch because my father made it a point to drop by the house late Saturday afternoon and take me to Mass, which fulfilled my Sunday obligation. Church was important to him, so I made it important for me.

During high school, I helped administer the sacrament of holy communion with the consecrated bread and wine. I continued that role when I left home for William & Mary, but my faith journey took off on a higher trajectory when I started attending a chapel service on Friday nights before our college football games.

That's where I heard chaplains describe the importance of having a personal relationship with Jesus. Scripture was clear on this, they said: Because God loved me, He cared about me regardless of what I'd done, where I'd been, or where I was headed. If I called on His name and sought Him in my life, He promised He would make Himself known to me.

College is when I really started to deepen my faith in God, but that journey took a detour when my father died suddenly in 1992. I was twenty years old at the time and really thrown for an emotional loop. I questioned my faith and wondered if God really understood how abandoned I felt or what I was going through after losing my dad. We had been getting along so well. His daily letters in my dorm mailbox stoked the fires of our close relationship.

And now he'd been taken from me.

God used two men in my life to snap me out of my spiritual low. The first was my high school football coach Warren Wolf. During one of his bye weeks, he drove seven hours to William & Mary to watch me play and have dinner afterward. When he said goodbye for the long drive home, we shook hands, but there was a folded-up bill pressed in his palm.

"Take it," he said. "I know you can use it."

I looked at the $100 bill. "No, Coach, I can't—"

"That's okay, Todd."

With that, Coach turned on his heels, and I watched him head off to his car. High school football coaches weren't given anything more than a modest stipend, but Coach Wolf knew I didn't have any money. He blessed me at a time when I could really use a hundred bucks.

The other person who impacted my spiritual walk was the late Father Charles Kelly, a campus minister at William & Mary. He hung out with the football guys and knew my dad because we'd see him at Mass when my father was in town.

After Dad died, Father Kelly took me under his wing. He talked to me about death, counseled me on what I needed to be prepared for in the wake of that tragedy, and listened to my questions. After an appropriate amount of time had passed from my father's burial, Father Kelly said he had a proposition for me: Would I like to join a college group traveling to Haiti during spring break and help out a sister parish?

I hadn't traveled much before, unless you count driving up and down the Atlantic seaboard as a globe-trotting experience. I'd certainly never been out of the country, so I needed a passport. When I heard that it wouldn't cost me a thing to go to Haiti because funds had been raised to send me and two dozen others to this poverty-stricken Caribbean island, I realized that I didn't have a good objection. I had to go.

I suffered from a bit of culture shock when our team landed in Port-au-Prince, the capital of the poorest country in the Western Hemisphere. We piled into several beat-up trucks and drove through shanty neighborhoods with slit trenches holding the stench of raw sewage.

What did I get myself into?

The streets were teeming with women walking with baskets of fruit and food on their heads. Boys and men led small herds of goats and the occasional cow. Local kids played in the sewer trench. We passed shacks where young mothers held babies in their arms with two or three kids tugging at their long dresses. There had to be families of eight, ten people living in lean-tos no bigger than my dorm room.

We drove forty miles into the jungle, which took five or six hours because we had to travel pothole-strewn dirt roads and ford swollen rivers. Once we arrived at the village, we were led to a shack. I was shown my bed—several slats of wood on a dirt floor. Meals for the next week would be beans and rice or rice and beans.

The village gathered for a church service upon our arrival. These were people who knew how to get their worship on. For three hours, they danced in the aisles, singing praises to the Lord and showing a spirit that I had never seen before. These people were so poor—and yet they were so rich in God's Spirit. This helped put life into perspective for me. I was reminded that no matter how bad things got for me, someone always had it far worse. Seeing how little they had was sobering, but I saw how much they praised God for the lives He'd given them!

That week in the Haitian jungle got my mind right. I'll never forget my return to the school campus in Williamsburg, Virginia, and noticing how people were rushing from one thing to another. Did they have toothy smiles like I saw everywhere in Haiti? No. When my friends complained about hitting a red light or not having a favorite dessert in the cafeteria, that hit me in a different way.

It took me the better part of a year to reach this point following my dad's death. I realized that I had to rely on my faith in God to get me through the day and that I was not guaranteed anything on this place called Planet Earth. My mind needed to be fixated on a far greater place awaiting me. Heaven would be a place where all my pain and anguish would be taken away.

Until that happens and I meet Jesus face-to-face, though, God had a job for me, which was to spread the good news and impact others to follow Him by doing good.

These days, when I speak to business groups and fitness experts, I've become much bolder about saying God's name. Part of that comes from feeling more comfortable about my faith, and part of it is gratitude: God has been so faithful to me and my family over the years. It's hard to dismiss His work in my life just because it may not be politically correct to mention His role in my existence.

And I've gotten more confident in the way I speak these days. People ask me afterward, "Where is this energy coming from?" or "Where is that light coming from?" I can't discount the impact that working closely with Dr. Jeremiah three times a week has had on my life either.

I've always been on point when I speak before an audience on the Xs and Os of training, success, significance, impact, and purpose. And purpose for me will always be God's purpose for my life, which comes out naturally and authentically.

I never want to alienate anyone who's not a believer, and I respect all people and their views. I just realize that the more obedient

WHAT WOULD JESUS DO?

Here are the questions I ask myself on a regular basis to keep my mind right:

- What would Jesus do if He was in this situation?
- How would Jesus coach this athlete or client?
- How would Jesus be a teacher?
- How would Jesus lead this Mastermind group?
- What would Jesus say in this talk today to motivate and bring people together and not ostracize them?
- What would Jesus be like as a parent?
- How would Jesus handle a difficult leadership challenge at work?
- If Jesus was an athlete, what would He be like?
- If Jesus was my training partner, who would He be like?

I like keeping questions like these in the forefront of my mind. When I do, my mind is right and I know that I can tap into the whispers.

I am to my calling and purpose, the more my purpose and calling is revealed and deepened. I also believe that all people yearn for something far greater than themselves.

And I haven't been proven wrong yet.

AS IRON SHARPENS IRON

Have I told you how much I love speaking at high school assemblies?

Talk about people who are yearning for something greater. There's something about the energy of several hundred spirited high school kids that I can feed off when I get rolling into my talk. Unlike some of my keynote talks to buttoned-up business groups where I have to be more reserved than I like to be, I can give student audiences an extra dose of energy.

I was once speaking to six hundred students at a local high school. I dove right in with one of my all-time favorite *Rocky* quotes. "'Let me tell you something you already know. The world ain't all sunshine and rainbows,'" I bellowed at the start of my talk. "'It's a mean and nasty place that will knock you to your knees and keep you there permanently if you let it. You, me, or nobody is gonna hit as hard as life! But it ain't about how hard you get hit. It's how hard you can get hit and keep moving forward. That's how winning is done.'"

Okay, a good opening. I looked around the auditorium to see how I was being received. I wouldn't say that I had the students in the palm of my hand yet, but my opener was solid. I then told them I'd be sharing five things that make up a champion's mindset.

"The first thing is that when God made us, God don't make junk!" I roared, not using the right verb conjugation on purpose to cut through the clutter.

I was working my way through my five bullet points—sharing ideas on how to dream big, be the hardest worker in the room, be tough and overcome adversity—when I opened my Bible to Proverbs 27:17.

"This is perhaps my favorite verse in the Bible," I said. "'As iron sharpens iron, so one man sharpens another,' says this verse from Proverbs." And to make sure that the young women in the auditorium didn't check out because of the masculine terms, I added this: "So a woman sharpens another as well."

Fifteen minutes into my presentation, I was thinking, *These kids are hanging with me. They're engaged.* Even though I talk a million miles an hour, I'm reading a crowd all the time. I'm making mental notes along the way, calibrating how I'm doing and what I'm going to say next since I generally speak without notes.

And that's when I noticed a young man—probably a sophomore or junior—leaning back in his chair, head tilted to the heavens, and eyes closed. He was sleeping soundly. Dead to the world. Splayed out in the ninth or tenth row.

Now there's something you should have figured out by now regarding me: I don't abide slackers—in the gym, on the field, or in my audience, even though I couldn't recall anyone ever falling asleep before.

This jump-started an internal dialogue within me:

Do I go over and wake him up while I'm walking around?

Do I point this kid out and embarrass him to kingdom come?

Is my talk that boring to put a kid to sleep? There's no way that's possible!

But then I had a check in my spirit. Maybe the kid didn't get any sleep the previous night because he had to study or finish a project. Maybe his mom and dad were fighting. Maybe he has something going on that I don't know about. Do I call him out anyway?

These were the fleeting thoughts that darted around my mind as I glanced a second and third time to see if he was still sleeping. Yup, he was still catching flies with his mouth wide open. Thank goodness he wasn't snoring.

"Listen up—no one wants to go through pain," I said to the assembly. "Some of you today are facing trials and tribulations. You're making decisions."

And then this thought hit me: here was a perfect opportunity for me to make a point about "iron sharpening iron" with this young man.

I stopped what I was doing and pointed to a teen boy sitting next to this young man sleeping. "Hey, time-out. Do me a favor. Wake that kid up," I said. "I need him up."

A few snickers rippled through the auditorium. I bet they hadn't seen this before in a school assembly.

A nudge in the ribs startled the teen. His eyes popped open—only to notice that everyone in the auditorium was staring at him. I locked eyes with him.

"That's it. Give me your eyes," I said. "I need you up. That's called iron sharpens iron. I'm sharpening you up. I'm not letting a brother down. I need you to hear this."

And that's all I said to him. I looked elsewhere to take the spotlight off this boy and resumed my talk. "If today you need strength, need to be lifted up, you need courage, then know this: lean on your faith. Pray to God and say, 'Dear God, please help me. I want to be a vehicle for You. Please work through me. I promise that I will do everything I can do to honor You in all that I do, and the choices I make and the decisions I make.'

"I know it's going to be tough, but today, if you're feeling challenges at home, in sports, in school, and in life, you got people bullying you, you have to know that you can overcome adversity. You can overcome that through God. You can overcome that by having mentors in your life. Iron sharpens iron."

And that's what "iron sharpens iron" is all about—having mentors, teachers, coaches, teammates, or friends in your life who can get your mind right. Even though you won't find the word *mentor* in the Bible, it's modeled several times in Scripture. We see Jesus mentoring His disciples. Barnabas mentoring Saul after he was blinded by a bright light on the road to Damascus. Saul taking the name of Paul and mentoring Timothy.

216

This is why I always say you're going to be better off surrounding yourself with thoroughbreds, not donkeys. You want to be around people who are motivated to do great things.

The greatest mentor in my life, save for my father, was Coach Wolf, my high school football coach, who passed away in November 2019. The guy was a coaching legend for the Green Dragons—which is the greatest team name in the world. He was Brick's first football coach when the high school opened in 1958 and he had the Midas touch. His teams were always one of the best in the state. For *fifty-one years* he coached Brick's football teams and had only three losing seasons. Thirteen times his Green Dragons won the New Jersey state title or the equivalent.

My older brother Paul was the quarterback when Coach Wolf won his first state championship in 1974. I wish I had been old enough to appreciate what a big deal that was, but I was a toddler playing with other kids under the grandstands.

When I got older, I dreamed of donning the green-and-white uniform and the helmet with the University of Michigan–style wings and leading my team down the field, heaving long touchdown passes or running through the secondary on my way to a game-winning score. I wanted to play for Coach Wolf because his teams won so many championships, and if I played well, perhaps I could win a college scholarship. I knew my divorced parents didn't have the money to pay for college.

I was in eighth grade when Coach Wolf took a keen interest in me. Coach always kept an eye out for the kids coming up—that was one reason his teams were always winners. He was coaching for today and he was coaching for tomorrow. When he heard that I was tearing it up on the Pop Warner team and made an All-American team, he took me under his wing.

Toward the end of my eighth-grade year, he offered to pick me up after school and drive me over to Brick High, where he supervised passing drills between his would-be varsity quarterbacks and receivers. I couldn't have been happier to be included in that group.

I let him coach me up. He worked on my footwork, reading the secondary, throwing balls to spots, and carrying out fakes in the daunting Wing-T offense. I soaked up everything he said. In his midsixties with a shock of grey hair, floppy hat, khaki pants, and high-top leather football cleats, Coach Wolf was a throwback, an old-school football coach in the Vince Lombardi mold.

Coach Wolf took "iron sharpens iron" seriously. He lived it at every practice. I believe that if I was sitting in an audience and fell asleep like that kid in the assembly, Coach Wolf would have done the exact same thing: he would have woken me up and told me he was doing this for my own good, as "iron sharpens iron."

I know it would be a lesson I'd never forget.

FINAL CALL

Hey, tapping into your whispers is not easy. It requires you to sit in silence and listen. I can't encourage you to do that enough. Sometimes the whispers are quiet. Sometimes they are loud. Just keep tapping in and being obedient to what they are saying.

I have a strong faith. And I'm always working to make it stronger. Being a man of faith does *not* make me perfect, however. Nor does my faith make me better than anyone else. Instead, it gives me a divine purpose far greater than myself alone. My faith gives me purpose to live and make this world a better place.

This is as much as I've ever shared publicly about my faith before. But it's who I am. While I never want to turn nonbelievers away, a big part of who I am *is* because of my faith. Prayer, getting in a good Bible-based church, finding a small group to have Bible study with, and tapping into your whispers are imperative when you're working on your spiritual life too.

Don't be afraid of religion. Develop a relationship with Jesus, and then it's between you and Him. At the end of the day, that's all that matters. Go deep and listen intently. God will direct your ways.

And then tap into the whispers!

Live a Life Worth Telling a Story About

The purpose of life is a life of purpose.
—Robert Byrne, author

When Devon Cassidy and I were eliminated in Week 3 of the NBC reality show *Strong*, filming didn't wrap up until 2:00 AM.

I marched straight to the training room, which resembled a MASH unit. It's a wonder I got there under my own power because my body was so beat up. Welts covered my arms, and there were scratches on my legs. Everything hurt—my back, my shoulders, my knees, and every muscle in between.

I was ticked that we lost. I don't like losing, especially when a national audience is looking on. I felt like I wasn't able to show what was truly inside of me, which left me upset, frustrated, and disappointed.

I took a physical inventory. Where I hurt the most was my right shoulder, which felt like it was on fire. I knew exactly when I had injured it: doing the first obstacle in the Elimination Tower. After a running start, Devon and I were tasked with jumping and hanging on to a large wishbone-shaped bag, but we needed enough momentum to cross a ten-yard chasm to the other side before we could go on to the next obstacle.

Devon, a twenty-four-year-old career woman from Boston, was unhappy, unhealthy, and not in a good place when she picked me as her trainer; that's what she told the cameras following us everywhere. In three weeks, I did what I could to get her in better shape, but inside the Elimination Tower that night, she couldn't hang on to the oversized leather bag when we tried to get to the other side.

She fell off probably a dozen times, forcing us to start over again each time. With the competition slipping out of reach, we had a moment.

"I'm so tired," she whispered, clearly defeated.

"I know you are. Let's just get across this. Come on, you can do this," I encouraged her.

"No, I don't think I can." Devon's shoulders sagged.

"Yes, you can. Positive self-talk. We got this. One more try. Let's get it on *this* one right here."

She must have listened because a look of fierce determination came across Devon's face. She would give it another try.

Knowing that it was now or never to stave off elimination, that's when I said to myself, *Screw it*, and pinned her to the bag—and tore something in my shoulder. Ouch!

We somehow made it across the moat, a minute behind the Gray team of Wes Okerson and trainee Jasmine Loveless. We never caught up, but we fought for small victories. After the Gray team had won, we were still working our way up the Elimination Tower. Devon was struggling to cross the rotating coil ladder, which resembled a long set of monkey bars. Even though we had already lost, she wanted to complete this obstacle.

Midway through, though, she was stuck. "I can't!" she cried out.

"Yes, you can!" I countered while waiting for her on the other side. "I believe in you!"

Devon struggled to hang on to the bars, but to her credit, she didn't give up. One by one, swinging from one bar to the next, she managed to get close enough to me so that I could pull her in. When her awesome effort was over, I drew her close and clasped her in a hug. She fell into my arms and let loose a jumble of tears: she had done something that she thought was impossible.

"Thank you," she said, sniffling. "There's nobody else I'd rather do this with."

I sensed this was a life-changing moment for Devon. "You were scared as heck today, you beat yourself up mentally, but look at what you did," I said. "You proved to yourself that you can do this. Don't let anybody tell you that you can't do something. The power is within you!"

"This has been the most amazing experience," Devon said, her voice still cracking. "You changed my life."

"No, *you* changed your life, Devon." I drew her in for one more affirming hug. "I'm so proud of you."

We heard host Gabby Reece tell us, "Unfortunately, Devon and Todd, the game is over for you."

Inside the training room afterward, a physician looked over my purple-splotched shoulder, which was painful to the touch and looked like a bruised peach. "Looks like you tore something. You'll want to get that checked when you get back home."

I grimaced and glanced up to see Dave Broome, *Strong*'s executive producer. After getting an update from one of the trainers, he approached my examination table. "Valiant effort," he said. "You were awesome. America's going to see the fight that you put up and the level of coach you really are."

I mumbled some sort of thanks.

"Hey, stay ready," he continued. "There might be an opportunity to get back in the game. There's always a twist."

A twist? "What do you mean by that?"

"I can't explain everything right now, but just stay ready."

"Well, I'm going home to see my family and check on my business. Plus I jacked my shoulder, as you can tell."

There wasn't much more to say. While the losing women trainees were obligated to stay on the set of *Strong* to continue working out as part of their body makeovers, the trainers were free to go home. It wasn't a good idea for me to drive home in the middle of the night, so I returned to my room to get a few hours of shut-eye.

CHANGING THINGS UP

Driving south on the 405 to San Diego the following morning, a Wednesday, I stewed over my early exit from *Strong*. While I was stuck in traffic, I called Warren Roark, a close college buddy of mine who always made me laugh when I was down. I told him I was no longer on the show.

Warren looked at the bright side. "Hey, maybe you got enough airtime so that it will be good for your brand," he said. I doubted it.

And then he said something else. "Don't worry about it. They will probably call you back to go on the show again and knowing you, you'll go back and win the whole thing."

Now that made me laugh!

I didn't phone Melanie. I decided I'd surprise her when she got home from work in the afternoon, before the kids arrived from school. Thinking about the five long weeks without seeing my family nearly reduced me to a puddle of tears on the side of the road.

I got home safely. In the middle of the afternoon, I heard the garage door go up. I peeled off my shirt and stood in the door. When Melanie spotted me, she nearly drove into the house. She slammed the car into park and hustled out to give me the warmest hug and kiss.

Then she stepped back and appraised me from head to toe.

"What the heck happened to you? What's with all the cuts and bruises? What did they do to you? And why are you home?"

"We lost last night. I got eliminated. The cuts? Let's just say it was pretty rough out there." That was the understatement of the day.

"Oh, honey. You're going to need to see a doctor."

And that's what I did. I had an orthopedic surgeon friend, Dr. Damion Valletta, who got me in the next day for an appointment and MRI. He told me I had torn the labrum in my right shoulder, which is the cartilage that keeps the ball of the shoulder joint in place. He said my labrum was 50 percent torn and that we could schedule a surgery that would take place in two to three months, or we could just wait to see how the shoulder was in a couple months and then make a decision to undergo surgery.

I told him I'd wait.

Two days later, I was standing on the sideline of my son Luke's Pop Warner football game as both teams were warming up. I was excited to be back to coaching and resuming some normalcy in my life.

My phone rang. I looked at the number. Dave Broome, the executive producer of *Strong*, was calling.

Why was he calling me on a Saturday morning just a few days after I got eliminated from the show? I had to satisfy my curiosity.

"Todd, I got Sylvester on the line with us."

The gruff voice of *Rocky* greeted me. "Hey, Todd. Howya doin'?"

Strong was Sylvester Stallone's show as much as it was Dave Broome's. I got the chance to meet Stallone on set and shared what a big fan I was. And I remembered seeing him after we lost in the Elimination Tower, which had Stallone's handprints all over it.

"Not so good," I allowed. "I just saw my doc. I tore my labrum, my right knee is shot, and my back is crushed."

"Sorry about that," Stallone said.

"Yeah, you laid it all on the line," Broome added. "But listen. We need you back up here. There's an opportunity to get back in the game."

"Get back in the game?" I refuted. "I don't think you understand—"

"Listen, come back up here. We'll get you back on TV. If you can't compete, at least you'll get on another episode, but we do need you back up here."

I had always been a team player. "Okay," I heard myself saying. "When do you need me?"

"Monday."

Melanie thought I was either crazy or a glutton for punishment to return to the set of *Strong* in Malibu.

On Monday morning, as I prepared to leave for Malibu, I had an early breakfast with the family before heading up to the set. I asked each of them, "Who thinks Dad has a chance to get back in this game?"

Melanie laughed. "Not a chance."

Luke chuckled as well. "Good luck, Dad, but I'll be seeing you on Wednesday. We need you to coach Pop Warner."

McKenna was just as adamant. "Dad, no way," she said.

But my middle child, Brady, said this: "Dad, you got this. They have no idea what's inside of you, and I believe in you. I think you are going to go out and shock the world."

Now it was my turn to laugh. But that's all I needed—one of the four to believe in me.

"Thanks, Brady. I'll see you guys in a few weeks."

Out the door I went, headed to Malibu and into the unknown.

Once there, I found out I'd be competing against three of the four other trainers who'd been eliminated. One trainer, Adam Von Rothfelder, injured his leg and was not medically cleared to compete in the "comeback challenge." Only one of us would get back into the game, and we would be paired with one of the five women who'd been eliminated up to that point. All of us would be returning to the Elimination Tower for the comeback challenge, and all of us would be going through the Elimination Tower solo.

I still wasn't sure if or how I was going to compete in the comeback challenge. And hearing that the way to win was going to be running through the Elimination Tower solo brought equal parts fear and a smile to my face. I was the one who had coined it the "Opportunity Tower" early in the game. Now there was a golden opportunity right in front of me. And I wasn't about to let Brady down either. I just had no idea how I was going to pull it off.

I remember walking around the grounds that day and overhearing conversations from the five trainers still in *Strong*. I kept hearing names like Drew and Leyon being tossed out as likely to get back into the game; never once did I hear my name.

I took it personally. Hearing them talk that way made me mad and put some vinegar in my blood. The five trainers still in the game had become friends, and none of them believed I could beat out the other three. They and the rest of the world hadn't seen what I had inside my gut.

That afternoon, my mindset changed from *There's no way I'm competing because my body is jacked up* to *Somehow I'm going to find a way to win tonight and shock the world.*

My mind was absolutely right.

Before dinner, I went for a walk in the hilly rural property set in the Santa Monica Mountains. I looked up and saw two huge boulders on a hillside. I sat down on a nearby bench and began to pray. I sat there for about twenty minutes and then something happened to me that had never happened before.

As I stared at those two boulders, I saw my dad's face and Ken Sawyer—my good buddy Saw Man—staring down at me as clear as day. They had ear-to-ear smiles on their faces and kept saying in unison, *We got this tonight. We got this tonight.*

Then my father looked down at me with the most loving and compassionate expression. *I'm proud of you, but the best is yet to come,* he said. *You're going to show the world what you're all about. I know what's inside of you because I've been watching closely. I'm going to help you tonight.*

225

I choked up hearing my father's words. The three trainers I would be competing against had no idea what was coming at them. Not only was my mindset stronger, but my injured shoulder was miraculously feeling much better. Something was happening here.

That night at the Elimination Tower, with dozens of technicians running about and cameramen setting up all over the place, I was grateful that it was just me going into the tower. I wanted the responsibility of winning or losing on my own shoulders.

Leyon Azubuike was first. Twenty-nine years old, six feet four, and 250 pounds of chiseled muscle, Leyon was a massive man who reeked of pure athleticism, strength, and power. He was Jennifer Aniston's boxing trainer—and also the youngest *Strong* trainer. I had no doubt he was the strongest.

He moved through the tower quickly, but he did some of the obstacles incorrectly, like using his upper body instead of his whole body to propel a weighted platform with him on it, from the first floor to the second floor of the tower. That move fatigued his arms for the next obstacle—the rotating coil ladder. He fell off the first time, losing valuable seconds.

Drew Logan was next. Another stud, Drew had somehow survived three cardiac arrests in the same afternoon five years earlier, so I knew he was a comeback guy. He raced through the Elimination Tower in 2:33, which was an awesome time even though I noticed that he had lost several seconds when he stopped to adjust his gloves before attacking the coil ladder and stopped to take three deep breaths right after finishing the coil ladder. Still, 2:33 was the time to beat. I knew that was lightning fast.

I was up next. I must have looked dazed by Drew's fast time, because another trainer, Chris Ryan, pulled me aside.

"Todd, don't forget who you are," he said, nearly punching a hole in my heart with his finger. "You're Todd 'Freakin' Durkin."

"Oh, yeah, you're right," I said. My mind was right now.

I snapped my IMPACT band. It was GO time. In the darkness at the base of the Elimination Tower, I focused on the task at hand.

We got this. We got this. I felt my heartbeat coming through my shirt. In the stillness, I reminded myself, *Whatever you do, don't stop when you're in the tower.*

The starting bell sounded, and I don't remember feeling a thing. Suddenly, I was twenty-five years old again, absolutely flying through the first of six obstacles—the double-wishbone bag. Then I hoisted my bodyweight up from the first floor to the second floor with my entire body, and not just with my upper body like Leyon did.

I flawlessly rolled the "steamrollers" without a hiccup, and before I knew it, I was climbing up a ladder to the third floor, where the dreaded coil ladder was waiting for me.

I reminded myself *not* to stop and take three breaths like Drew did.

Suck it up and keep going.

I jumped out on the coil ladder and started to traverse the twenty-foot-long rotating coil. Because my right shoulder was so banged up, I bent my arms at 90 degrees and kept my head close to the ladder.

Before I knew it, I was on the other side of the ladder. I dropped on the platform but reminded myself again to not catch my breath for a moment.

Go, go, go. Don't stop.

I got to the "Mousetrap," which required me to crawl on my hands and knees and lift a half-dozen heavy platforms off my back as I traversed up to the fourth and final floor. These platforms were supposed to be heavy, but it felt like Dad and Saw Man were lifting them for me.

I arrived at the fourth floor and had no idea what my time was. I just knew I was still flying. I stepped up on top of the Strong Tower with my legs quivering. Without missing a beat, I started pulling on a rope that lifted circular blocks with the letters *S*, *T*, *R*, *O*, *N*, and *G* to the top of a two-story column. I slipped, which ended up being a blessing as I dug my heels into a half-inch lip on a steel grate. This allowed me to get more strength with each pull. One by one, each letter cinched in place, and before I knew it, I finished.

The all-out exertion took every ounce of energy I had within me. I lay down on the steel grate and literally saw my chest pounding. I had just laid it all on the line.

Was my time good enough? I wasn't sure. Win or lose, there was no way I could have done the Elimination Tower any better.

After catching my breath, I heard host Gabby Reece call my name.

I walked over to the side of the fourth floor of the Elimination Tower and looked down about ninety feet to the ground. She was standing next to all the trainers and trainees, each with expectant looks on their faces.

Gabby looked up to me. "Todd, that was an epic run. Drew had the time to beat at 2:33. And that time was as good as we have seen. Your time was . . ."

Everything moved into slow motion. I saw my kids' faces at the breakfast table. I saw Melanie's face smiling as she kissed me goodbye. I heard the voice of my buddy Warren saying, "You're probably going to find a way to get back in the game and win this thing." And I heard my dad's and Saw Man's voices saying, *We got this.*

"Your time was two minutes aaannnnddddd thiiirrrttty seconds!"

Wait a second . . . I was trying to do the math in my head. Then it clicked: 2:30 was less than 2:33.

Did I just beat Drew? Did I just get back in the game?

I had! You betcha that was a faster time. I pounded one fist into another in exaltation. But I hadn't won yet. There was still one competitor to go, Ky Evans.

Ky gave it his best shot, but he ran into trouble and couldn't finish the Elimination Tower, meaning I was back in the game.

Gabby made it official. "Todd Durkin, you are the comeback trainer back on *Strong.* Congratulations, and get ready to compete with your new partner," she announced.

I went bananas. I didn't care that it was 2:00 AM again. I just remember shouting out at the top of my lungs, "DRAAGOOOO! DRAAGOOOO!"

I was paying homage to my boyhood hero Rocky Balboa when he was preparing to fight Russian heavyweight boxer Ivan Drago in *Rocky IV* and just ran up a massive mountain in Siberia, raising his arms in exultation.

I laughed to myself and thought, *Melanie and the kids aren't going to believe this!*

MEETING MY NEW *STRONG* PARTNER

A half hour later, I was paired with the winner of the trainee side: Brittany Harrell-Miller, who had quite a backstory as well. She was a seventh-grade math teacher in her midtwenties who'd been through hell and back.

Brittany had grown up in a broken home and mothered a child when she was a junior in high school. She juggled single parenthood with her college education in mathematics at the University of Kansas. She earned her teaching credential and was educating junior high students in her math classes. She lived in Lawrence, Kansas.

I loved Brittany's fight and immediately jelled with her. We kept winning, and in the weeks we found ourselves with our backs to the wall in the Elimination Tower, we discovered something extra within ourselves to survive another week.

But here's what viewers of *Strong* never saw. Each "week" was really three days: a challenge, followed by another challenge the next day, followed by the Elimination Tower. Every single day of the week we were competing, and every third day we seemed to find ourselves in the "Opportunity Tower" again.

We were getting physically annihilated. Whupped. But we kept winning and staying in the competition. When our backs were against the wall—literally and figuratively—we showed up.

I remember pleading my case with the director. "Listen, this is inhumane. We've got to get some rest. Can we get one day off?"

The director placed an arm on my shoulder. "Listen, man. We're behind budget. We have a timetable and have to get this wrapped up by Thanksgiving."

It's too bad I couldn't show him Key #8 on the importance of recovery, but I was stuck.

Those were the cards we were dealt. I saw Brittany's mindset change as well regarding the Elimination Tower. "We'll just keep whipping butt," she said, and that's what we did.

Brittany and I kept coming back until we found ourselves in the final "week" of *Strong*, pitted against former Dallas Cowboys strength and conditioning coach Bennie Wylie and Minnesota mom Jill May, a pastor's wife and mother of four. Together, they were a formidable pair—a combination of grit, experience, and integrity.

I couldn't work up any us-versus-them animosity against them. They were solid Christians with incredible attitudes about life. In the final episode of *Strong*, Bennie and Jill beat us the first night when they won an obstacle course by thirteen seconds. They were given the choice of receiving $50,000 or five seconds off their time in the Elimination Tower. If they lost to us in the tower, however, they wouldn't get to keep the money. Bennie and Jill chose the five-second time advantage when they faced us for the grand finale. That was the ultimate sign of respect.

The following day, Brittany and I engaged in an old-fashioned tug-of-war and then had to transfer 20-pound kettlebells from the top of our pyramid to the top of their pyramid while racing up and down a set of stairs. We won the tug-of-war and the kettlebell race and were given the same option by Gabby Reece: $50,000 or five seconds in the Elimination Tower.

This was a no-brainer: we chose the five-second time advantage, which meant we would be going into the Elimination Tower even-steven with Bennie and Jill. The winning team in the tower would receive the prize money they had accrued during the show. Bennie and Jill were competing for $300,000. Brittany and I were competing for $200,000. The losing team would get nothing.

On the afternoon of the final competition, the four of us were walked through the Elimination Tower as part of a safety check. After six trips to the tower (in just ten weeks), I knew the obstacles fairly well. This time, though, the producers were changing some of the obstacles. The wishbone bag, for instance, was replaced with a "battering ram" and a wall that had to be knocked down. I didn't see a problem with that.

But on the second level, a four-piece stairway was replacing a set of steamrollers. We would have to push each piece of stairway to the next piece. When we pushed three pieces of stairway into the fourth piece, we would be driving 700 pounds up a slight grade until all four pieces locked into a wall and allowed us to move on.

When I saw what the *Strong* producers had done to this obstacle, I knew our chances of winning were over. My battered body didn't have any juice left, and Brittany had suffered a bone bruise a few days earlier in Week 8 when a large panel came down on her foot during the Elimination Tower challenge. She had summoned everything she had to get us through Week 9 in the tower, but she wasn't anywhere near 100 percent.

"There's no way," I said to her, out of earshot of Bennie and Jill as well as the *Strong* producers. "Let's just go out there and enjoy this."

Now, I know what you might be thinking: *Todd, you gave up.*

No, I didn't, and neither did Brittany. We both had an understanding that we had gone on *Strong* for something greater than us: I was there for all the trainers who grind from 5:00 AM to late at night and never get a shot like this; Brittany for all her algebra students at Liberty Memorial Central Middle School in Lawrence, her eight-year-old son, Jadin, and all their friends in the Sunflower State.

Spoiler alert: The 700-pound stairway proved to be our undoing, and we lost by sixteen seconds. Like I said, I knew going in that we couldn't beat Bennie and Jill because we were injured. No shame in that. When it was all over, I felt total relief. I had never been purely motivated by winning up to $500,000 in prize money.

Now I could go home with my head held high and let my pummeled body recover. I was down to 188 pounds and looked like I'd taken beatings from sadistic prison guards with billy clubs.

But I had been able to show the world what was on the inside and how I competed for a purpose way greater than just me.

Eight months later, I brought Brittany and Jadin out to San Diego to join us at a watch party held at Fitness Quest 10 on June 2, 2016, with all our friends and colleagues. We both knew the result of *Strong*'s final episode, of course, but we were legally bound not to disclose the outcome to friends and family. Even though our loss was aired to America, we were still winners when the credits ran.

Like I said, it was never about the money but about meeting the physical and mental challenges that the *Strong* producers threw at us. We proved to ourselves, our communities, and the people who watched the show that we had what it took to compete and compete well.

Because we were living lives worth telling a story about.

YOU CAN FINISH STRONG TOO

When you came into this world, your life was like a book filled with blank pages. Everything you've done so far has been recorded, but from this day forward, it's up to you what you fill the rest of the pages with. Will your life be worth reading about someday? Are you living a life worth telling a story about right now?

I wouldn't be surprised if you have overcome difficult challenges in the past. Perhaps your parents divorced when you were young, like my mom and dad did, or you're a single parent like Brittany. Perhaps you were bullied in school or tormented on social media while growing up. Perhaps you were abused as a child or as an adolescent. I can only imagine how horrible these stories are and how hard it is to talk about them—or even recall them.

Maybe you got through your teenage years okay but had to drop out of college because the funds weren't there. Maybe you worked your butt off to get your degree only to find you couldn't get hired in the profession you were counting on to pay your student loans. What have you overcome to get where you are today? Or are you still trying to figure out what to do in life? That's okay, too. We're all on a journey.

Or maybe you recently lost your job or suffered a setback in your career. Maybe you're in a career transition and "starting over" again. Perhaps you're facing a tough time financially and trying to figure out how to get out of a deep hole of debt. Or maybe a relationship or marriage has gone south, or you've suffered a divorce.

STOP.

Today is a new day. Don't let any negative self-talk—or what I call "head trash"—keep you from your destiny. It's time to fulfill your purpose, starting today. You have so much future ahead of you, and when you get your mind right, you can accomplish goals that you never thought possible.

Several years ago, I decided to sponsor a contest at Fitness Quest 10 and called it "Live a Life Worth Telling a Story About—What's Your Story?" I offered a $1,000 cash prize to the person who shared the most inspirational story.

We had dozens and dozens of entries, well over one hundred. I read every single one and learned a great deal about my clients. I was also reminded that there was pain and adversity beyond the walls of Fitness Quest 10 that I knew nothing about.

One person wrote that she was nearly killed in a car accident and endured months of difficult rehab. Another overcame drug addiction and was doing amazing things with her life. A father described the emotional impact of losing an adolescent son in a car crash. Staff Walker, a client in his seventies, said he was in the

US Marine Corps and became a city bus driver after his honorable discharge. He had never mentioned this before in all the years we worked together.

One evening at Fitness Quest 10, we held a reception where I announced the winner—Tim Kahlor, who worked at the University of California, San Diego. His story detailed his massive personal challenges over several years: a son wounded in Iraq; a wife paralyzed from the waist down in a 2009 accident; a brother and a sister with early-onset Parkinson's disease; a sister who had survived a bout of breast cancer; and a brother who passed away in 2008. He said he was burned-out but wanted to be healthier and feel better about himself, and that's where I came in. He said I inspired him to change his mindset, but it really was the other way around. Tim Kahlor and his amazing story was inspiring me to inspire others.

What I remember most about Tim is that he donated the $1,000 cash prize back to my Impact Foundation, which really choked me up. Talk about paying it forward. That special evening reminded me that everyone has a story to share, and their stories are filled with ups and downs, with triumphs and tragedies.

Just to be clear here: I believe everyone has a life worth telling a story about. And you may not realize this, but you're writing your story right now.

Since each day we get to write that story is a gift—something we all need to be reminded of often—go make it a good one.

FINAL THOUGHTS

For the last time, I'm going to take you through the principles—the keys—I've shared in this book:

- realize that how you think determines your life and your legacy;
- run toward your fears and attack them;
- establish your best practices;

- use exercise, nutrition, and recovery as part of your game plan; and
- recognize the importance of creating a champion mindset.

You can use all of these keys to craft the most amazing life based on your divine purpose.

I often hear this question from people: "How many keynote talks do you do a year?"

Here's my answer: "Every day I'm giving myself a keynote. It starts when I get my early morning routine in and do my quiet time. All my journaling, introspection, and self-talk is like giving myself a keynote."

When I'm done with my morning routine, I'm fueled up and fired up for the day because I've taken the time to get my mind right. That's when I can go out and share my energy with the world and live a life worth telling a story about.

There's no reason why you can't have an extraordinary life as well. Establish good habits, rules to follow, best practices—and then maniacally follow them. Realize that change doesn't come overnight but strive to get 1 percent better every day. And tell someone you know well—a spouse, a partner, a teammate, a colleague, or a close friend—that you have a new attitude about life and are going to get your mind right physically, mentally, and spiritually.

Once you do, you'll be well on your way.

And I'm predicting that you'll have some amazing stories worth telling.

One more thing: the next time you're facing an obstacle, challenge, or situation in life that seems daunting or too big, remember that it is an *opportunity* to get stronger and better, just like the Elimination Tower was an opportunity for me to stay on *Strong.* You are always way stronger than you think.

After all, you don't know how strong you are until strong is all you have left.

Until next time . . . GET YOUR MIND RIGHT!

ACKNOWLEDGMENTS

The bigger your dream, the more important your dream. And when you have a big dream and you want to pour your heart and soul into a project, there are a lot of people who help make it happen. *Get Your Mind Right* was a labor of love, and I have tremendous gratitude for the many people who made it possible.

First, I'd like to thank my collaborator, Mike Yorkey. Before every meeting or phone interview, we always prayed together for God's divine wisdom and intervention, which I believe is evident throughout the book. Mike was an absolute joy to work with, and I appreciate his wisdom, skill, and ability to help me put the right words on paper.

Next, I'd like to thank my literary agents at Park & Fine Literary and Media. Sarah Passick, Anna Petkovich, and Celeste Fine, you are the best. You believed in me from the start, and I remember us talking about the "missing part" I needed to share when we were brainstorming this book. I'm glad that discussion came up so that I could openly share my faith in God and how He impacts me in everything I do. I look forward to impacting many people with you all in the years to come.

I have huge gratitude to the great people at Baker Books. I remember being interviewed by a couple of editors just five days after my partial knee replacement. I was sitting in my recliner, icing my knee with a Game Ready, and sharing my passion to help people get their minds right. In other words, I was getting my mind right at the exact time we were discussing what *Get Your Mind Right* would look like!

From that first interview after my surgery, to the meeting in Portland, and to our multiple discussions, I have been honored to work with the amazing Baker team that starts with Rachel Jacobsen and includes Patti Brinks, Eileen Hanson, and Wendy Wetzel. I hope this is just the beginning for us.

A special thank-you to our editor, Meredith Hinds. Every great book has a great editor, and Meredith did an excellent job making the original manuscript shine even more.

A huge thanks to my team, clients, and members at Fitness Quest 10, starting with Julie Wilcox and Jeff Bristol, who kicked me out of the gym on my "writing days" to make sure I stuck to my deadlines. And a massive thank-you to Larry Indiviglia for helping me outline *Get Your Mind Right* and recall many of my stories and their minute details. Larry makes me and our team better on all levels every day. I'm also grateful for everyone who helps me get people's minds right on the *Todd Durkin IMPACT Show* podcast: Amelianne Johannes, Jess Jacobsen, Zach Sperrazzo, and Kayla Barber. Each week, they help me create and produce content to help change people's lives.

To all my Todd Durkin Mastermind members who I get to coach on a regular basis, I'm blessed to have some of the most inspiring and impactful coaches around the globe in my Mastermind group. All of you inspire me to be better every day. Thank you for giving me the opportunity to coach and lead you.

To all the MindRight Maniacs around the globe who inspire me on a daily basis, please know that I read all your DMs, tweets, and emails. It's your daily messages that keep me inspired and motivated to deliver my life's purpose. Thank you and keep them coming!

Turning to my family, my wife, Melanie, has helped me beyond expectations with her ideas, input into the content of the book, and editing every chapter. I'm thankful and blessed to have Melanie as my wife and value her support and belief in me. Finally, I want to thank my kids, from whom I stole too many evening and weekend hours to complete this book. Luke, Brady, and McKenna give me their love, support, and patience as Daddy tries to change the world. Having a deep purpose is one of the most important things in life, and so is time with your kids. Blending the two and balancing it all out is one of the hardest tasks there is. You guys inspire me every single day, and I love you to the moon and back forever.

ABOUT THE AUTHORS

Todd Durkin, MA, CSCS, is an internationally recognized strength and conditioning coach, bodyworker, author, and motivational speaker. He is the founder of Fitness Quest 10 in San Diego, California, an award-winning health and human performance facility where he works with a high-profile clientele of elite professional athletes—including NFL MVPs, Super Bowl champions, Heisman Trophy winners, MMA world champions, Olympic and X-Game gold medalists, and World Series champions.

Fitness Quest 10 has been named one of "America's 10 Best Gyms" by *Men's Health* five different times. Durkin's work has earned him the industry's highest honors, including "Personal Trainer of the Year" by both IDEA and ACE. He has been named among the Top 100 Most Influential Persons in Health & Fitness four times and was the 2017 Jack LaLanne Award winner, representing legacy and impact in the fitness industry.

Since 2007, Todd has hosted his own retreats and mentorships and currently leads the Todd Durkin Mastermind Group for high performers seeking growth in business, leadership, branding, and personal development. Todd has an award-winning podcast, *The Todd Durkin IMPACT Show*, which is guaranteed to get your mind right each and every week.

Durkin is the author of two previous books: *The IMPACT! Body Plan* (Rodale Books, 2010), a ten-week, comprehensive plan to change body, mind, and spirit; and *The WOW Book: 52 Ways to Motivate Your Mind, Inspire Your Soul & Create WOW in Your Life* (CreateSpace, 2016).

He lives with his wife, Melanie, and their three children, Luke, Brady, and McKenna, in San Diego. They have a five-year-old golden retriever named Jersey who accompanies them on many of their workouts.

Mike Yorkey is Todd Durkin's collaborator. A veteran author or coauthor of more than one hundred books, he has collaborated with Casey Diaz, a former Latino gangbanger, in *The Shot Caller*, and Ron Archer, an inspirational African American preacher, in *What Belief Can Do*, and is the coauthor of the internationally bestselling *Every Man's Battle* series with Steve Arterburn and Fred Stoeker.

His website is www.mikeyorkey.com.

INVITE TODD DURKIN
TO SPEAK TODAY

Todd Durkin is a dynamic keynote speaker who loves inspiring those seeking high performance and maximum success in their life. He has spoken all over the world to a wide array of audiences in a multitude of industries.

As one committed to creating a massive impact, Todd has a passion to instill a championship mindset in people of all ages, levels, and sectors. He has a knack for tapping into people's mindsets and heart-sets to help them reach their full potential personally and professionally. His passion, contagious positive energy, and ability to connect with all audiences allow him to routinely receive standing ovations and rave reviews.

If you, your business, your conference, your college or university, or your organization would be interested in having Todd speak, please contact him via email at durkin@fitnessquest10.com, phone at (858) 271-1171, or through his website at www.todddurkin.com.

For bulk purchases of *Get Your Mind Right*, please contact Todd at durkin@fitnessquest10.com.

FOLLOW TODD DURKIN
ON SOCIAL MEDIA

If you'd like to stay connected to and motivated by Todd Durkin, be sure to subscribe to his award-winning podcast, *The Todd Durkin IMPACT Show* on iTunes, Stitcher, Spotify, or Google Play and listen to his "get your mind right" messages. New episodes come out every week.

Additionally, you can opt in to his free "Dose of Durkin" at www.DoseOfDurkin.com, where he delivers motivational and inspirational messages directly to your phone or email address every Monday morning to help get your mind right for the coming week.

You can also follow Durkin on the following social media apps:

- Instagram at @ToddDurkin
- Facebook fan page at ToddDurkinFQ10
- Twitter at @ToddDurkin
- LinkedIn at Todd Durkin
- YouTube: ToddDurkinFQ10

SOURCE MATERIAL

Key #1 Dream Big—and Attack Your Fears!

35: "Life ain't about how hard ya hit . . ." is from "Rocky Balboa Motivational Speech to His Son," Goalcast.com, April 15, 2016, https://www.goalcast.com/2016/04/15/rocky-balboa-motivational-speech-son/.

36: BHAG—big, hairy, audacious goals—was coined by Jim Collins in Jim Collins and Jerry I. Porras, *Built to Last* (New York: HarperBusiness, 1994).

Key #2 Your Thoughts Ultimately Determine Your Legacy

55: "Make sure your worst enemy . . ." is from "Laird Hamilton Quotes," Goodreads, https://www.goodreads.com/quotes/7834156-make-sure-your-worst-enemy-doesn-t-live-between-your-own.

Key #3 Life Requires You to Overcome Obstacles

69: "Success is not to be measured . . ." is from "Booker T. Washington Quotes," Goodreads, https://www.goodreads.com/quotes/963031-success-is-not-to-be-measured-by-the-position-someone.

81: "So many of our dreams at first seem impossible . . ." is from "Christopher Reeve Quotes," Goodreads, https://www.goodreads.com/quotes/13050-so-many-of-our-dreams-at-first-seem-impossible-then.

83: "You've got to be very careful if you don't know where you are going . . ." is from "Yogi Berra Quotes," Goodreads, https://www.goodreads.com/quotes/266663-you-ve-got-to-be-very-careful-if-you-don-t-know

Key #4 Habits Will Make or Break You

89: "Discipline is the bridge . . ." is from "Jim Rohn Quotes," Goodreads, https://www.goodreads.com/author/quotes/657773.Jim_Rohn.

98: Caffeine study by researchers at the Sleep Disorders & Research Center is from Christopher Drake et al., "Caffeine Effects on Sleep Taken 0, 3, or 6 Hours before Going to Bed," *Journal of Clinical Sleep Medicine* 9, no. 11 (2013): 1195–1200, http://jcsm.aasm.org/viewabstract.aspx?pid=29198.

99: Effects of the use of electronic devices before bed is from "Why Electronics May Stimulate You Before Bed," National Sleep Foundation, https://www.sleepfoundation.org/articles/why-electronics-may-stimulate-you-bed.

100: Gallup poll result is from Frank Newport, "Most U.S. Smartphone Owners Check Phone at Least Hourly," Gallup, July 9, 2015, https://news.gallup.com/poll/184046/smartphone-owners-check-phone-least-hourly.aspx.

Key #5 Be a Master of Your Time, Energy, and Focus

107: "One reason so few of us achieve . . ." is from Tony Robbins, quoted in Dan Scalco, "22 Time Management Quotes to Inspire You to Achieve Your Goals," Sept. 28, 2017, https://www.inc.com/dan-scalco/22-time-management-quotes-to-inspire-you-to-achieve-your-goals.html.

108: "Most of us are just trying to do the best that we can . . ." is from Jim Loehr and Tony Schwartz, *The Power of Full Engagement: Managing Energy, Not Time, Is the Key to High Performance and Personal Renewal* (New York: Simon & Schuster, 2003), 3.

109: National study by Asurion is from SWNS, "Americans Check Their Phones 80 Times a Day: Study," *New York Post*, Nov. 8, 2017, https://nypost.com/2017/11/08/americans-check-their-phones-80-times-a-day-study/.

109: Average screen time for adults is from Quentin Fottrell, "People Spend Most of Their Waking Hours Staring at Screens," MarketWatch, Aug. 4, 2018, https://www.marketwatch.com/story/people-are-spending-most-of-their-waking-hours-staring-at-screens-2018-08-01.

110: Research by Common Sense Media is from Jenny Anderson, "Even Teens Are Worried They Spend Too Much Time on Their Phones," Quartz, Aug. 23, 2018, https://qz.com/1367506/pew-research-teens-worried-they-spend-too-much-time-on-phones/.

110: Average worker productivity is from Melanie Curtin, "In an 8-Hour Day, the Average Worker Is Productive for This Many Hours," Thrive Global, Apr. 25, 2018. https://thriveglobal.com/stories/in-an-8-hour-day-the-average-worker-is-productive-for-this-many-hours/.

111: Time to refocus, according to Gloria Mark, is from Blake Thorne, "How Distractions at Work Take Up More Time Than You Think," *I Done This* (blog), July 23, 2015, http://blog.idonethis.com/distractions-at-work/.

111: *Journal of Social and Personal Relationships* study is from Bruce Weinstein, "Distractions Are Killing Your Career, and They'll Kill You Too," *Forbes*, June 25, 2018, https://www.forbes.com/sites/bruceweinstein/2018/06/25/distractions-are-killing-your-career-and-theyll-kill-you-too/#5f8dfdafa305.

111: Distracted driving statistics are from "Distracted Driving 2016," National Highway Traffic Safety Administration, April 2018, https://crashstats.nhtsa.dot.gov/Api/Public/ViewPublication/812517.

119: *Wall Street Journal* report is from Daniela Hernandez, "How Smartphones Sabotage Your Brain's Ability to Focus," *Wall Street Journal*, May 16, 2019, https://www.wsj.com/video/how-smartphones-sabotage-your-brains-ability -to-focus/72E56EB0-0B92-44BF-9897-08461040E3E8.html.

119: Cal Newport, *Digital Minimalism: Choosing a Focused Life in a Noisy World* (New York: Portfolio/Penguin, 2019).

Key #6 Train to Win

135: "I hated every minute of training . . ." is from Muhammad Ali, "Training Quotes," BrainyQuote, https://www.brainyquote.com/topics/training.

142: "A sound body . . ." is from Thales of Miletus, quoted in Aspa Giannopoulou, "A Sound Mind in a Sound Body," Greek Blogyssey, April 26, 2012, https://blogs .fco.gov.uk/aspagiannopoulou/2012/04/26/a-sound-mind-in-a-sound-body/.

145: Muscle, fat, and bone mass facts are from Susan Brady, "5 Important Reasons to Maintain Lean Body Mass as You Age," Virginia Therapy & Fitness Center, Feb. 15, 2018, https://www.spinemd.com/vtfc/news/5-important-reasons -to-maintain-lean-body-mass-as-you-age.

153: "A coach is someone who tells you . . ." is from Tom Landry, quoted in Susan Merrill, "Our Top 10 Favorite Tom Landry Quotes," All Pro Dad, https:// www.allprodad.com/our-top-10-favorite-tom-landry-quotes/.

155: "I could never have won all those championships . . ." is from *Wooden's Wisdom*, https://www.woodenswisdom.com.

Key #7 Eat Right to Get Your Mind Right

157: "Let food be thy medicine . . ." is from Hippocrates, quoted in Richard Smith, ed., "Let Food Be Thy Medicine," *BMJ* 328 (Jan. 24, 2004): 7433, https://www.ncbi.nlm.nih.gov/pmc/articles/PMC318470/.

163: Sugar consumption facts are from "How Much Sugar Do You Eat? You May Be Surprised," National Health Service, Aug. 2014, https://www.dhhs.nh.gov /dphs/nhp/documents/sugar.pdf.

169: National Institutes of Health study on brain fog is from Umberto Volta et al., "An Italian Prospective Multicenter Survey on Patients Suspected of Having Non-Celiac Gluten Sensitivity," *BMC Medicine* 12 (May 23, 2014), https://www.ncbi.nlm.nih.gov/pubmed/24885375/.

174: Fact about bacteria in gut is from "NIH Human Microbiome Project Defines Normal Bacterial Makeup of the Body," National Institutes of Health, June 13, 2012, https://www.nih.gov/news-events/news-releases/nih-human-micro biome-project-defines-normal-bacterial-makeup-body.

Key #8 Recovery Will Get Your Body and Your Mind Right

179: "Life's a marathon . . ." is from "Phillip C. McGraw Quotes," Goodreads, https://www.goodreads.com/quotes/341222-life-s-a-marathon-not-a-sprint.

182: "Sleep plays a major role . . ." is from Dr. James B. Maas, quoted in Daniel G. Amen, *Change Your Brain, Change Your Body* (New York: Harmony, 2010), 195.

183: Gallup Poll on hours of sleep is from Jeffrey M. Jones, "In U.S., 40% Get Less Than Recommended Amount of Sleep," *Gallup News*, Dec. 19, 2013, https://news.gallup.com/poll/166553/less-recommended-amount-sleep.aspx.

185: Studies on blue light exposure is from "Blue Light and Your Eyes," Prevent Blindness, https://www.preventblindness.org/blue-light-and-your-eyes.

186: "Sleep is something that I have talked about . . ." is from "Tom Brady Replaces High-End Mattress with a Bed-in-a-Box," *Boston Globe*, Aug. 28, 2018, http://realestate.boston.com/style/2018/08/28/tom-brady-sleeps-on -bed-in-a-box/.

187: "I'm pretty sure there is some effect . . ." is from Jeff Barker, "Tom Brady Is Under Armour's 'Muse' on New Athlete Recovery Line," *Baltimore Sun*, May 26, 2017, https://www.baltimoresun.com/business/bs-bz-under-armour -sleep-studies-20170526-story.html.

189: Midday nap study is from Christopher Lindholst, "Feeling Burned Out at Work? There's a Nap for That!," Thrive Global, May 1, 2019, https://thrive global.com/stories/feeling-burned-out-at-work-theres-a-nap-for-that/.

189: Nap study in *Behavioural Brain Research* is from Sara C. Mednick et al., "Comparing the Benefits of Caffeine, Naps and Placebo on Verbal, Motor and Perceptual Memory," *Behavioural Brain Research* 193, no. 1 (Nov. 3, 2008):79–86, https://www.sciencedirect.com/science/article/pii/S016643280 8002416.

196: Cryotherapy at French Open is from Simon Cambers, "Chill Out Rafa: Why Nadal, Stars, Are Turning to Cryotherapy," ESPN.com, June 8, 2019, https://www.espn.com/tennis/story/_/id/26925743/why-nadal-stars-turning-cryo therapy.

Key #9 Tap into the Whispers

214: "Let me tell you something . . ." is from Sylvester Stalone, "Rocky Motivational Speech to His Son," Rocky in *Rocky Balboa* (Beverly Hills, CA: MGM Distribution, 2006).

215: Proverbs 27:17 quoted from the BSB version.

Key #10 Live a Life Worth Telling a Story About

219: "The purpose of life . . ." is from "Robert Byrne Quotes," Goodreads, https://www.goodreads.com/quotes/1429-the-purpose-of-life-is-a-life-of-purpose.

CONNECT WITH TODD

TODD DURKIN
PASSION · PURPOSE · IMPACT

ToddDurkin.com

 ToddDurkinFQ10

  ToddDurkin

TUNE IN TO TODD'S
PODCAST

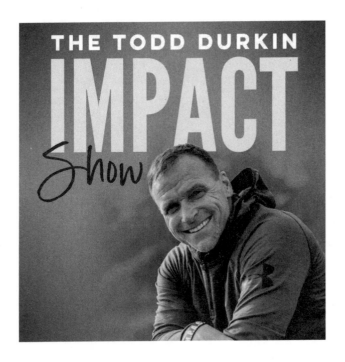

The Todd Durkin IMPACT Show is designed to motivate and inspire you to live a life full of passion, purpose, and IMPACT. It's guaranteed to **GET YOUR MIND RIGHT**. The IMPACT Show is for anyone who seeks high performance in business, sports, leadership, or life.

Available Wherever You Get Your Podcasts